DEFENDERS
OF THE
PLANTATION
OF
ULSTER
1641-1691

Muster Roll of the Garrison of Londonderry
during the Rebellion of 1642-1643

Defenders of Ireland during the
Williamite War of 1689-1691

Compiled by
BRIAN MITCHELL

CLEARFIELD

Copyright © 2010
by Brian Mitchell
All Rights Reserved.

Printed for Clearfield Company by
Genealogical Publishing Company
Baltimore, Maryland
2010

ISBN: 978-0-8063-5456-9

Made in the United States of America

INTRODUCTION

DEFENDERS OF THE PLANTATION OF ULSTER 1641-1691

The Plantation of Ulster

In the 17th century substantial numbers of English and Scottish families settled in the northern part of Ireland during the so-called Plantation of Ulster. The Province of Ulster consists of the counties of Antrim, Armagh, Down, Fermanagh, Londonderry and Tyrone in Northern Ireland and of the counties of Cavan, Donegal and Monaghan in the Republic of Ireland.

The defeat of the old Gaelic order in the Nine Years War, 1594-1603 and the escape of the most prominent Gaelic Lords of Ulster in 'the Flight of the Earls' in 1607 from Lough Swilly, County Donegal were ultimately responsible for the settlement of many English and Scottish families in the northern counties of Ireland.

Movement of Scottish settlers in a private enterprise colonisation of counties Antrim and Down began in earnest from 1605 when Sir Hugh Montgomery and Sir James Hamilton acquired title to large estates in north Down and Sir Randall MacDonnell, 1st Earl of Antrim, to large tracts of land in north Antrim.

In 1609 the Earl of Salisbury, Lord High Treasurer, suggested to James I a more formal, deliberate plantation of Scottish and English colonists on the forfeited estates of Gaelic chiefs in counties Armagh, Cavan, Donegal, Fermanagh, Londonderry (then known as Coleraine) and Tyrone. It was felt that the only way to deal with Ulster, described as "the most rude and unreformed part of Ireland and the seat and nest of the last great rebellion" was the creation of a new settlement strong enough to resist the native Irish.

These settlers came to Ulster, by and large, in three waves: with the granting of the initial leases in the period 1605 to 1625; after 1652 and Cromwell's crushing of the Irish rebellion; and finally in the fifteen years after 1690 and the Glorious Revolution.

By the end of the 17th century a self-sustaining settlement of English and Scottish colonists had established itself in Ulster. It is estimated that by 1715, when Scottish migration to Ulster had virtually stopped, the Presbyterian population of Ulster, i.e. of essentially Scottish origin, stood at 200,000.

Londonderry, Coleraine, Carrickfergus, Belfast and Donaghadee were the main ports of entry into the province of Ulster for 17th century British settlers with the Lagan, Bann and the Foyle valleys acting as the major arteries along which the colonists travelled into the interior.

Scottish families entering through the port of Londonderry settled in the Foyle Valley which includes much of the fertile lands of counties Donegal, Londonderry and Tyrone. The lands along the Firth of Clyde in Ayrshire; the Clyde Valley; Wigtown, Kirkcudbright and Dumfries in Galloway; and the Border Lands of Berwick, Peebles, Selkirk and Roxburgh were home to many of these Scottish settlers.

INTRODUCTION

English settlers, mostly drawn from the northern counties of Cheshire, Cumberland, Lancashire, Northumberland, Yorkshire and Westmorland tended to favour settlement along the Lagan Valley in the east of the Province.

The importance of Londonderry during the Plantation of Ulster

The 'island' of Derry, bounded to the north, east and south by the River Foyle and to the west by the 'Bogside', a deep channel carved out by glacial meltwaters at the end of the last ice age, was to assume a vital role in safeguarding the 17th century Plantation of Ulster as it attempted to establish itself in a hostile environment.

By tradition, St Columcille, also known as St Columba, founded a monastery at Derry, in 546 AD, on the crest of small, wooded hill on the west bank of the River Foyle. For the next one thousand years Derry was a monastic centre of some importance.

Owing to Derry's central position between the two most powerful Gaelic kingdoms of the O'Neills of Tyrone and the O'Donnells of Donegal, it was only a matter of time before the English crown, who had been attempting to pacify Ireland throughout the 16th century, would attempt to fortify Derry. The patent rolls of James I, dated 11 July 1604, states "the town or borough of Derry is by reason of the natural seat and situation thereof, a place very convenient and fit to be made both a town of war and a town of merchandize".

To ensure the success of the Plantation in North West Ireland, the government decided to involve the City of London and its mercantile wealth (as opposed to wealthy individuals, known as undertakers, in the other Plantation counties) in the important area of the north coast between the River Foyle and River Bann.

In January 1610 the City of London finalised its contract with the crown, agreeing to the plantation of the entire county of Londonderry (created formally in 1613) as well as to a specific town-building programme at Derry and Coleraine.

The Honourable The Irish Society, composed of "six and twenty honest and discreet citizens of London", was formally constituted by Royal Charter of James I on the 29th March 1613 to direct the affairs of the plantation. This charter also defined and established the City and County of Londonderry.

The construction of a fortified settlement on the island of Derry was an essential aspect of the Plantation. Defence of the quayside was paramount as Londonderry city was to be both a point of entry for development of the Londoners' plantation and as a place of ultimate refuge in times of difficulty. Such roles were possible only if access to the River Foyle could be kept secure.

Construction of the walls began in 1614. By May 1619, Captain Nicholas Pynnar, Inspector of Fortifications in Ireland, was able to report that the city walls, with a circumference of 5124 feet, had been completed. He found a strong stone wall, 24 feet high by 18 feet thick, defended by 9 bulwarks, 2 half-bulwarks and 4 battlemented gates. He also recorded 92 houses containing 102 families which he considered 'far too few a number for the defence of such a circuit'.

INTRODUCTION

Londonderry was now ready to play its pivotal role in safeguarding the settlement of 17th century English and Scottish planters in Ulster as its walls repulsed Sieges in 1641, 1649 and 1689.

Identifying Early Planters

The names of some 2,500 planters who played their part in defending and securing the Plantation of Ulster during the 1641 rebellion and the Williamite War of 1688 to 1691 are identified in two sources, namely:

- Muster Roll of Garrison in City of Londonderry, 1642-1643
- *Fighters of Derry Their Deeds and Descendants* by William R Young

Tables, in alphabetical order by surname, of these 2 sources are included in this book. This now makes the identification of the 17th century Planters of Ulster much easier.

Table 1: Muster Roll of Garrison in City of Londonderry, 1642-1643

Throughout the 17th century, landlords mustered their tenants periodically to identify able-bodied men capable of military service. Most of the names in these rolls are of Planter or British origin, although a few native Irish names are also recorded.

On 22 October 1641 the native Irish, under Sir Phelim O'Neill, rose in rebellion in Counties Londonderry and Tyrone, and the walled city of Londonderry became a refuge for Protestant settlers. A "League of the Captains of Londonderry" was set up to guard the city, with the raising of nine companies of foot soldiers, each assigned with a particular section of the walls of Derry to repair and to defend. By April 1642 the city was close to starvation, with the rebel forces led by Sir Phelim O'Neill camped at Strabane. However, the threatened siege of Derry was lifted on 17 May 1642 by the defeat of the Irish army, led by the O'Cahans (O'Kanes), near Dungiven by an army consisting of east Donegal settlers and four Companies of soldiers from Londonderry.

The 'Muster rolls of foot companies in the garrison of Londonderry', dated May 1642-August 1643 (Public Record Office of Northern Ireland, T808/15176; taken from National Archives, London, State Papers Domestic, Commonwealth Exchequer Papers, bundles 120 and 121), names 905 men in 9 foot companies, consisting of 90 officers and 815 soldiers, who defended Derry's walls during the siege of 1641/42:

Company Commander	Date of Muster	Officers	Soldiers
Sir John Vaughan	19 May 1642	10	100
Jasper Hartwell	20 September 1642	10	53
Henry Finch	18 August 1643	10	87
Thomas Newburgh	18 August 1643	10	84
Sir Thomas Staples	18 July 1643	10	100
Tristram Berisford	18 July 1643	10	100
Robert Thornton	18 August 1643	10	99
Henry Osborne	18 August 1643	10	100
John Kilner	18 August 1643	10	92
Total		**90**	**815**

INTRODUCTION

These men would have been drawn from estates throughout County Londonderry and neighbouring counties and, if called upon, they would have defended the walls of Derry with the cannons that were sent to the city in May-June 1642 by the Livery Companies of the City of London. Seven of these cannon are now restored and are located on Derry's Walls today at the following locations:

Type of Cannon	London Company that sent the Cannon	Location
Demi-culverin	Salters	Artillery Bastion
Demi-culverin	Merchant Taylors	Church Bastion
Demi-culverin	Merchant Taylors	Church Bastion
Demi-culverin 'Roaring Meg'	Fishmongers	Double Bastion
Demi-culverin	Vintners	Double Bastion
Demi-culverin	Grocers	New Gate Bastion
Demi-culverin	Mercers	New Gate Bastion

(Note: A demi-culverin is a type of cannon with a bore averaging 4.5 inches and firing a shot of 9-12lbs.)

The 1659 Census of Ireland provides clues as to the place of residence of the soldiers who served in the foot companies as it records the names of "Tituladoes", i.e. the principal persons of standing in any particular locality; such a person could have been a nobleman, landowner, military officer or adventurer. In most cases the person of standing in a district was the landowner. Landowners, in raising companies of foot soldiers, would have recruited from the tenantry on their estates.

The 1659 Census appears to record the following 'tituladoes' in County Londonderry who raised regiments for the defence of Londonderry in 1641/1642:

Titulado	Parish	Locality
Henry Osborne	Templemore	Silver Street (now Shipquay Street), Londonderry city
Henry Finch	Templemore	Diamond, Londonderry city
Henry Finch junior	Faughanvale	Longfield Beg and Tullybrisland
John Kilner	Faughanvale	Muff (the village was renamed Eglinton in 1858)
Tristram Beresford	Coleraine	Coleraine town and Liberties

It would also appear that three of the commanders of foot companies raised during the 1641 rebellion were property holders inside the walled city of Londonderry in 1628. The Rent Roll for the city, dated 15 May 1628 (published, by the Londonderry Sentinel in 1936, as *A Particular of the Howses and Famylyes in London Derry May 15, 1628)*, records the names of 155 leaseholders; three of whom were Henry Osborne, Robert Thornton and Sir John Vaughan.

INTRODUCTION

The table of the 1642/1643 Muster Rolls consists of 4 fields: Surname, First Name, Rank; and Foot Company.

An example of information provided against each entry is as follows:
Surname: Newcomb
First name   Thomas
Rank   Soldier
Company   Thomas Newburgh's Foot Company

Table 2: Fighters of Derry Their Deeds and Descendants

William R. Young's *Fighters of Derry Their Deeds and Descendants: Being a Chronicle of Events in Ireland during the Revolutionary Period 1688-1691* (published by Eyre and Spottiswoode, London, 1932) is a unique and unrivalled source for tracing 17th century Plantation ancestors. This book names and, in many cases, provides biographical detail of 1660 "Defenders" and 352 officers of the "Jacobite Army".

'Defenders' in Young's book refers to much more than just simply a list of those who were documented as playing their part in the defence of Londonderry during the famous Siege of Derry which commenced with the closing of its gates on 7 December 1688 and ended on 31 July 1689 with the Jacobite army in retreat after a relief fleet, with essential food supplies, managed to break through the boom of fir and iron cable across the River Foyle.

'Defenders' refers to all those people who were named in contemporary sources and accounts as playing an active or supportive role in the successful Williamite campaign of 1689 to 1691.

The Williamite War in Ireland, 1689-1691, was, in effect, the struggle for the English throne between the deposed James II, the last Catholic monarch of the three Kingdoms of England, Scotland and Ireland who had the support of Louis XIV of France, and William of Orange with the backing of the English Parliament.

The successful Williamite campaign included the defence of Derry during the Siege of 18 April to 31 July 1689; the harrying of Jacobite forces in Connaught and Ulster by locally raised regiments operating out of Enniskillen throughout 1689; victories at the Battle of the Boyne on 1 July 1690 and the Battle of Aughrim (County Galway) on 12 July 1691; and the final Irish surrender of Limerick on 23 September 1691.

As well as naming defenders of Derry, Young's book names those who were involved in the Enniskillen campaigns and in other battles such as the Boyne. It also names the prominent supporters of Protestant interests throughout Ireland at this time, including the identities of 921 people from Ulster who were declared traitors by James II's short-lived Dublin parliament of May 1689.

Finally, it is very evident in any examination of Young's book that many of the 'defenders' are first, second, third or fourth-generation descendants of Scottish, English and Welsh planters. In many cases,

INTRODUCTION

Young connects the 'defenders' of 1689-1691 to the original planters who settled in Ireland.

This table of Young's 'Defenders' is, in effect, a list of the major Planter families of the province of Ulster and it, furthermore, identifies in many cases their connection to the original planters from England, Wales and, in particular, Scotland.

The table of 'Defenders' in Young's book consists of 5 fields: Young's ID, Surname, First Name, Residence; and Remarks. Young's ID refers to the identity number used by William Young for the 'defender' in his book. With this number you can consult Young's book to verify or gain additional information about any 'defender' recorded in the database. In the Remarks column I have inserted biographical detail, where provided by Young, about a 'defender' and their planter origins in England, Scotland or Wales.

An example of information provided against each entry is as follows:

Young's ID:	45
Surname	Beresford
First Name	Sir Tristram
Residence	Coleraine, Co. Derry
Remarks	Grandson of Tristram, son of Michael Beresford of Orford, who was appointed agent for London City Companies in County Londonderry in early days of Plantation

Young's book, furthermore, identifies many landowners who raised armies from the tenantry and neighbours of their estates. These armies, drawn from planters throughout Ulster, then played an active part in the defence of Derry and Enniskillen. Examples of landowners who raised such armies (and noted in the remarks column of this database) included:

Captain William Babington (Young's ID 805) with estates at Urney, Co. Tyrone and Castle Doe, Co. Donegal
Colonel Kilner Brazier (605) of Rath, Co. Donegal
Captain William Grove (Young's ID 238) of Castle Shannaghan, Co. Donegal
Colonel Hugh Hamill (428) of Lifford, Co. Donegal
Francis Hamilton (1097) of Castle Hamilton, Co. Cavan
Michael Harrison (955) of Killultagh, Co. Antrim
Captain William Wishard (1331) of Clontivern, Co. Monaghan.

The range of sources consulted by William Young in compiling his list of 'Defenders' was extensive. It included:

Ulster People named on list of attainted in James' Dublin parliament

- James II's Parliament, which met in Dublin on 7 May 1689 and sat for three weeks, passed 'The Bill of Attainder' which confiscated estates and condemned without trial over 2,500 persons (of whom 921 were from Ulster) of high treason.

INTRODUCTION

Signatories to:

- Corporation of Derry's Commission of 1690
  (At the end of 1690, some 216 of the leading citizens signed a commission empowering 3 agents to press the Government in London for compensation for the losses and damages incurred during the siege)
- Address to King William after Relief
- Enniskillen address to King William

References recorded in personal accounts and books such as:

- Siege Diary of Captain Thomas Ash which was published in 1792
- 'Siege' account published, in 1689, by Governor George Walker, Episcopalian minister
- 'History of the Siege' published, in 1690, by Rev. John Mackenzie, Presbyterian minister
- Dr. Joseph Aicken's poem 'Londeriados', published in 1699, which details incidents and participants in the Siege
- Rev John Graham's 'DERRIANA; Consisting of A History of the Siege of Londonderry and Defence of Enniskillen in 1688 and 1689, with Historical Poetry and Biographical Notes' (published 1823)
- John Hempton's 'Siege and History of Derry' published in 1861
- Charles Dalton's 'English Army Lists and Commission Registers, 1661-1714' (6 vols, London, 1892-1904). Details officers granted commissions before 1727.
- William Trimble's 'The History of Enniskillen with references to some Manors in Co. Fermanagh' published in three volumes between 1919 and 1921.

In consulting Young's book readers should be aware of the following observations:

Young frequently refers to Scotland as N.B., i.e. North Britain. Seemingly, after the union of England and Scotland in 1707, parliamentary legislation for a time used "South Britain" and "North Britain" to refer to the two parts.

In 'the names of the attainted' (i.e. traitors to James II) County Donegal addresses are frequently recorded as Donegal or Londonderry and vice versa. Derry and Londonderry refer to the same place.

Young makes the following assumption that 'the names of the attainted' in the counties of Antrim, Donegal, Down, Londonderry and Tyrone who, if not refugees across the Channel in England or Scotland, took refuge in Derry during the siege and contributed to its defence; while those with addresses in the counties of Armagh, Cavan, Fermanagh, Leitrim and Monaghan who, if they didn't flee across the Channel, became refugees in Enniskillen and shared 'in the glories of the defence'.

Within one generation many of those who fought in the Williamite War in Ireland were emigrating to the colonies in North America.

INTRODUCTION

Speaking of the 1718 emigration to Londonderry, New Hampshire, the Professor of History at Williams College said in 1890 (*Coleraine in Georgian Times* by T H Mullin): "Those best off of all the passengers, the McKeens, the Cargills, the Nesmiths, the Cochrans, the Dinsmoors, the Moores and some other families were natives of Scotland whose heads had passed over into Ulster during the short reign of James II. These were covenanters. They had lived together in the valley of the Bann Water for about 30 years, in or near the towns of Coleraine, Ballymoney and Kilrea."

John Caldwell who was born in 1769 in Ballymoney, County Antrim wrote: "Among the survivors of the siege of Londonderry were my two great-uncles Thomas Ball and William Caldwell, who with various others (John Barr, Abraham Blair etc) principally from the townland of Ballywatick in the parish of Ballymoney, some of whom had shared with them the hardships of the siege, not liking the aspect of public affairs in their own country, sought an asylum in America, and in the year 1718 when their average age might be about 48 emigrated to Boston and from there made their way to Nutfield [afterwards called Londonderry]."

Brian Mitchell
24 September 2009

MUSTER ROLL
OF THE
GARRISON OF LONDONDERRY
DURING THE
REBELLION OF 1642-1643

DEFENDERS OF LONDONDERRY, 1642

Surname	First Name	Rank	Company
Adams	Thomas	Soldier	Sir Thomas Staples' Foot Company
Adams	William	Sergeant	Tristram Berisford's Foot Company
Alcorne	John	Soldier	Tristram Berisford's Foot Company
All	John	Soldier	Tristram Berisford's Foot Company
Allan	Christopher	Soldier	Henry Finch's Foot Company
Allan	Patrick	Soldier	John Kilner's Foot Company
Allane	Bartell	Soldier	Henry Osborne's Foot Company
Allecen	Andrew	Soldier	Sir Thomas Staples' Foot Company
Allecen	William	Soldier	Sir Thomas Staples' Foot Company
Allen	John	Soldier	Thomas Newburgh's Foot Company
Allen	John	Drummer	Robert Thornton's Foot Company
Allen	John	Soldier	Henry Osborne's Foot Company
Allen	George	Soldier	Henry Osborne's Foot Company
Allen	James	Soldier	Henry Osborne's Foot Company
Allester	John	Soldier	Thomas Newburgh's Foot Company
Allexander	James	Soldier	John Kilner's Foot Company
Allinson	William	Soldier	Jasper Hartwell's Foot Company
Anderson	James	Soldier	Thomas Newburgh's Foot Company
Anderson	William	Soldier	Robert Thornton's Foot Company
Andros	Charles	Soldier	Thomas Newburgh's Foot Company
Andross	Richard	Soldier	Thomas Newburgh's Foot Company
Andross	Teige	Soldier	Thomas Newburgh's Foot Company
Ankor	Dunkan	Soldier	Henry Osborne's Foot Company
Anktill	James	Soldier	Henry Osborne's Foot Company
Aplin	Robert	Soldier	Sir John Vaughan's Foot Company
Appleton	William	Soldier	Robert Thornton's Foot Company
Arbuckell	James	Soldier	Sir John Vaughan's Foot Company
Arbuckle	James	Soldier	Henry Osborne's Foot Company
Armstrong	Edward	Soldier	Thomas Newburgh's Foot Company
Ash	John	Corporal	John Kilner's Foot Company
Ash	John	Soldier	John Kilner's Foot Company
Ashdone	Allex	Soldier	John Kilner's Foot Company
Atkinson	Richard	Sergeant	Sir Thomas Staples' Foot Company
Atkinson	Thomas	Soldier	Sir Thomas Staples' Foot Company
Auberry	Charles	Soldier	Sir John Vaughan's Foot Company
Austen	Richard	Lieutenant	Tristram Berisford's Foot Company
Averell	Henry	Soldier	Sir John Vaughan's Foot Company
Babington	Mathew	Soldier	Thomas Newburgh's Foot Company
Babington	Edward	Soldier	Thomas Newburgh's Foot Company
Baker	John	Soldier	Robert Thornton's Foot Company
Bakon	William	Soldier	Tristram Berisford's Foot Company
Bale	William	Soldier	Sir John Vaughan's Foot Company
Ball	Richard	Soldier	Sir John Vaughan's Foot Company
Ball	Isley	Soldier	Jasper Hartwell's Foot Company
Balrige	James	Soldier	Sir Thomas Staples' Foot Company
Banckes	Thomas	Soldier	Sir John Vaughan's Foot Company
Barbard	John	Soldier	John Kilner's Foot Company
Barber	George	Soldier	Jasper Hartwell's Foot Company
Barnes	Robert	Soldier	Jasper Hartwell's Foot Company
Barnsly	Fra	Soldier	Sir John Vaughan's Foot Company
Barr	Micaell	Soldier	Robert Thornton's Foot Company
Barr	William	Soldier	Robert Thornton's Foot Company
Barr	John	Soldier	Henry Osborne's Foot Company
Barry	John	Soldier	Sir John Vaughan's Foot Company

DEFENDERS OF LONDONDERRY, 1642

Surname	First Name	Rank	Company
Barry	Thomas	Soldier	Sir John Vaughan's Foot Company
Barton	William	Soldier	Thomas Newburgh's Foot Company
Bastard	David	Soldier	Thomas Newburgh's Foot Company
Bastard	Charles	Soldier	Robert Thornton's Foot Company
Bateman	Miles	Drummer	John Kilner's Foot Company
Baux	John	Soldier	Sir Thomas Staples' Foot Company
Baylye	John	Soldier	Robert Thornton's Foot Company
Beames	Henry	Soldier	Henry Finch's Foot Company
Beaumont	Thomas	Drummer	Thomas Newburgh's Foot Company
Beggs	James	Soldier	Henry Osborne's Foot Company
Benderman	James	Soldier	Tristram Berisford's Foot Company
Berisfford	Randall	Soldier	Tristram Berisford's Foot Company
Berisford	Tristram	Captain	Tristram Berisford's Foot Company
Beyles	James	Soldier	John Kilner's Foot Company
Bishopp	Richard	Soldier	Robert Thornton's Foot Company
Blackborne	Robert	Soldier	Thomas Newburgh's Foot Company
Blany	Cormack	Soldier	Sir John Vaughan's Foot Company
Blany	John	Soldier	Thomas Newburgh's Foot Company
Bogge	John	Soldier	Sir Thomas Staples' Foot Company
Bohanan	John	Soldier	John Kilner's Foot Company
Boyd	John	Soldier	John Kilner's Foot Company
Boyd	Minian	Soldier	Henry Finch's Foot Company
Boyde	John	Soldier	Henry Finch's Foot Company
Boyde	George	Soldier	Tristram Berisford's Foot Company
Boyde	Andrew	Soldier	Robert Thornton's Foot Company
Boyne	William	Soldier	Jasper Hartwell's Foot Company
Bramstone	John	Soldier	Tristram Berisford's Foot Company
Bramstone	William	Soldier	Tristram Berisford's Foot Company
Brellahan	Peter	Soldier	Jasper Hartwell's Foot Company
Brisson	Charles	Soldier	Jasper Hartwell's Foot Company
Brome	Thomas	Soldier	Henry Osborne's Foot Company
Browne	Thomas	Soldier	Henry Finch's Foot Company
Browne	Edward	Soldier	Thomas Newburgh's Foot Company
Browne	Robert	Soldier	Thomas Newburgh's Foot Company
Browne	James	Soldier	Sir Thomas Staples' Foot Company
Browne	John	Soldier	Henry Osborne's Foot Company
Browne	John	Soldier	John Kilner's Foot Company
Burdist	Richard	Soldier	Robert Thornton's Foot Company
Burnell	Thomas	Soldier	Henry Finch's Foot Company
Burnes	Robert	Soldier	Robert Thornton's Foot Company
Burrell	Thomas	Corporal	Thomas Newburgh's Foot Company
Burrell	John	Soldier	Thomas Newburgh's Foot Company
Button	James	Soldier	Sir Thomas Staples' Foot Company
Byar	Hugh	Soldier	John Kilner's Foot Company
Cade	Thomas	Soldier	John Kilner's Foot Company
Cahan	John	Soldier	Tristram Berisford's Foot Company
Cahan	Hugh	Soldier	Tristram Berisford's Foot Company
Cahan	Brian	Soldier	Tristram Berisford's Foot Company
Cahan	Rory	Soldier	Tristram Berisford's Foot Company
Cahowne	Thomas	Soldier	Thomas Newburgh's Foot Company
Cambell	John	Sergeant	Jasper Hartwell's Foot Company
Camell	John	Soldier	Tristram Berisford's Foot Company
Camell	James	Soldier	Robert Thornton's Foot Company
Campbell	Robert	Soldier	Henry Osborne's Foot Company

DEFENDERS OF LONDONDERRY, 1642

Surname	First Name	Rank	Company
Campian	James	Soldier	Tristram Berisford's Foot Company
Canwell	Hugh	Soldier	Jasper Hartwell's Foot Company
Care	Cormack	Soldier	Thomas Newburgh's Foot Company
Carmihill	James	Soldier	Robert Thornton's Foot Company
Carr	Daniell	Soldier	Sir John Vaughan's Foot Company
Carter	John	Soldier	Tristram Berisford's Foot Company
Carye	Edmund	Ensign	Tristram Berisford's Foot Company
Casell	Richard	Soldier	Thomas Newburgh's Foot Company
Casell	Richard	Soldier	Thomas Newburgh's Foot Company
Caskey	John	Soldier	Jasper Hartwell's Foot Company
Chambers	William	Soldier	Sir John Vaughan's Foot Company
Chambers	John	Soldier	Thomas Newburgh's Foot Company
Chapman	Gregory	Soldier	Sir Thomas Staples' Foot Company
Chaptman	Cormack	Soldier	Robert Thornton's Foot Company
Chetwood	Thomas	Ensign	Jasper Hartwell's Foot Company
Chiles	John	Soldier	Tristram Berisford's Foot Company
Chosan	Andrew	Soldier	Henry Osborne's Foot Company
Christye	John	Soldier	John Kilner's Foot Company
Clanton	Barnard	Soldier	Thomas Newburgh's Foot Company
Clapone	John	Soldier	John Kilner's Foot Company
Clarke	Gilbert	Soldier	Jasper Hartwell's Foot Company
Clarke	John	Soldier	Sir Thomas Staples' Foot Company
Clarke	John	Soldier	Tristram Berisford's Foot Company
Clarke	Thomas	Soldier	Robert Thornton's Foot Company
Clarkson	Thomas	Soldier	Sir John Vaughan's Foot Company
Clarkson	Thomas	Soldier	Sir John Vaughan's Foot Company
Clarson	Thomas	Sergeant	John Kilner's Foot Company
Clayde	Mungoe	Soldier	John Kilner's Foot Company
Cloyde	John	Soldier	Robert Thornton's Foot Company
Clrencors	David	Soldier	Sir Thomas Staples' Foot Company
Cockbarne	James	Soldier	Henry Osborne's Foot Company
Coeks	Robert	Soldier	Robert Thornton's Foot Company
Cole	John	Soldier	Sir Thomas Staples' Foot Company
Cole	Thomas	Soldier	Robert Thornton's Foot Company
Colhoune	Robert	Soldier	Henry Osborne's Foot Company
Coluine	John	Soldier	Henry Osborne's Foot Company
Conoher	Dankan	Soldier	Tristram Berisford's Foot Company
Cooke	George	Lieutenant	Henry Finch's Foot Company
Cooke	George	Soldier	Thomas Newburgh's Foot Company
Cooke	Thomas	Soldier	Tristram Berisford's Foot Company
Coote	William	Corporal	Henry Finch's Foot Company
Cootes	Christopher	Sergeant	Henry Finch's Foot Company
Cornhill	James	Soldier	John Kilner's Foot Company
Corrion	Hugh	Soldier	Thomas Newburgh's Foot Company
Courtney	William	Drummer	Jasper Hartwell's Foot Company
Cowhowne	Thomas	Soldier	Thomas Newburgh's Foot Company
Cowper	Micaell	Soldier	Thomas Newburgh's Foot Company
Cox	John	Soldier	Sir Thomas Staples' Foot Company
Coyle	Edward	Soldier	Tristram Berisford's Foot Company
Crafford	James	Soldier	Robert Thornton's Foot Company
Crage	Thomas	Soldier	Sir Thomas Staples' Foot Company
Crakshank	Gilbert	Soldier	John Kilner's Foot Company
Craneen	Richard	Soldier	Henry Finch's Foot Company
Craveen	John	Soldier	Henry Finch's Foot Company

DEFENDERS OF LONDONDERRY, 1642

Surname	First Name	Rank	Company
Craven	Thomas	Soldier	Henry Finch's Foot Company
Craven	John	Soldier	Henry Finch's Foot Company
Crawfforde	Thomas	Soldier	Sir Thomas Staples' Foot Company
Crayton	Gilbert	Soldier	Jasper Hartwell's Foot Company
Croase	Thomas	Ensign	Sir John Vaughan's Foot Company
Crokett	John	Soldier	Henry Osborne's Foot Company
Crookshank	Joseph	Soldier	Sir Thomas Staples' Foot Company
Crukshanks	James	Soldier	Thomas Newburgh's Foot Company
Cuin	Daniell	Soldier	Tristram Berisford's Foot Company
Cuningham	James	Soldier	Henry Osborne's Foot Company
Cunningham	David	Soldier	Henry Osborne's Foot Company
Cunningham	William	Soldier	Henry Osborne's Foot Company
Curry	Daniell	Soldier	Sir Thomas Staples' Foot Company
Cutbertson	Robert	Soldier	Henry Finch's Foot Company
Cutbertson	James	Soldier	Henry Osborne's Foot Company
Cuthbertson	William	Soldier	Robert Thornton's Foot Company
Dane	John	Soldier	Jasper Hartwell's Foot Company
Daniell	John	Soldier	Thomas Newburgh's Foot Company
Daniell	James	Soldier	Thomas Newburgh's Foot Company
Danielson	John	Soldier	Sir John Vaughan's Foot Company
Davenport	John	Lieutenant	John Kilner's Foot Company
Davenport		Soldier	John Kilner's Foot Company
Davies	Rice	Soldier	Sir John Vaughan's Foot Company
Davis	Lewis	Soldier	Henry Finch's Foot Company
Davis	John	Soldier	Sir Thomas Staples' Foot Company
Davis	John	Soldier	Robert Thornton's Foot Company
Davis	William	Soldier	Henry Osborne's Foot Company
Davison	John	Soldier	Sir Thomas Staples' Foot Company
Delap	James	Soldier	Sir Thomas Staples' Foot Company
Dixon	Andrew	Soldier	Sir Thomas Staples' Foot Company
Dobson	John	Soldier	Sir John Vaughan's Foot Company
Dorne	John	Soldier	Robert Thornton's Foot Company
Dougharty	James	Soldier	Sir John Vaughan's Foot Company
Dougherty	Thomas	Soldier	Sir John Vaughan's Foot Company
Dowell	John	Soldier	Thomas Newburgh's Foot Company
Dowell	John	Soldier	Thomas Newburgh's Foot Company
Dowgall	John	Soldier	Henry Osborne's Foot Company
Downe	Alexander	Soldier	Sir John Vaughan's Foot Company
Downes	Robert	Ensign	John Kilner's Foot Company
Downinge	George	Ensign	Henry Finch's Foot Company
Duce	John	Soldier	Thomas Newburgh's Foot Company
Duglas	Brian	Soldier	Thomas Newburgh's Foot Company
Duglas	Robert	Soldier	Tristram Berisford's Foot Company
Dugleish	John	Soldier	Henry Finch's Foot Company
Dulap	John	Soldier	John Kilner's Foot Company
Dulapp	David	Soldier	John Kilner's Foot Company
Dunbar	George	Soldier	Tristram Berisford's Foot Company
Duncan	John	Soldier	Sir John Vaughan's Foot Company
Dunkan	John	Soldier	Tristram Berisford's Foot Company
Durdok	Thomas	Lieutenant	Thomas Newburgh's Foot Company
Dutton	Thomas	Soldier	Sir John Vaughan's Foot Company
Dutton	Peirce	Soldier	Robert Thornton's Foot Company
Dyllan	Anthony	Soldier	Jasper Hartwell's Foot Company
Edmonstone	Robert	Soldier	Tristram Berisford's Foot Company

DEFENDERS OF LONDONDERRY, 1642

Surname	First Name	Rank	Company
Edwards	Richard	Soldier	Henry Finch's Foot Company
Edwards	John	Soldier	Tristram Berisford's Foot Company
Eiden	Robert	Soldier	Thomas Newburgh's Foot Company
Elkes	John	Soldier	Tristram Berisford's Foot Company
Ellicock	Edward	Soldier	Jasper Hartwell's Foot Company
Elliott	Symon	Soldier	Sir John Vaughan's Foot Company
Ellis	John	Soldier	Tristram Berisford's Foot Company
Enallre	Morice	Soldier	Sir John Vaughan's Foot Company
Enche	John	Soldier	John Kilner's Foot Company
Enlish	William	Soldier	Henry Finch's Foot Company
Erwin	Richard	Soldier	Jasper Hartwell's Foot Company
Erwin	Edward	Soldier	Thomas Newburgh's Foot Company
Erwin	Walter	Soldier	Sir Thomas Staples' Foot Company
Erwine	Edward	Soldier	Thomas Newburgh's Foot Company
Erwine	Richard	Soldier	Sir Thomas Staples' Foot Company
Erwine	John	Soldier	Henry Osborne's Foot Company
Evin	Torby	Soldier	Robert Thornton's Foot Company
Ewin	Humphry	Soldier	Tristram Berisford's Foot Company
Ewrye	Robert	Soldier	Henry Finch's Foot Company
Eyers	John	Soldier	Sir John Vaughan's Foot Company
Ferrier	John	Soldier	Thomas Newburgh's Foot Company
Ferry	Mathew	Soldier	Sir Thomas Staples' Foot Company
ffinch	Henry	Captain	Henry Finch's Foot Company
ffinch	Hernry	Soldier	Henry Finch's Foot Company
ffinch	Henry	Soldier	Henry Finch's Foot Company
ffixter	William	Soldier	Henry Osborne's Foot Company
fflanell	John	Soldier	Henry Finch's Foot Company
ffleminge	James	Soldier	Henry Osborne's Foot Company
ffoker	James	Soldier	John Kilner's Foot Company
ffranckland	James	Soldier	Sir John Vaughan's Foot Company
ffulton	John	Soldier	Henry Osborne's Foot Company
ffulton	John	Soldier	John Kilner's Foot Company
Fleming	William	Soldier	Robert Thornton's Foot Company
Fleminge	David	Soldier	Tristram Berisford's Foot Company
Fleminge	John	Soldier	Henry Osborne's Foot Company
Folliott	Robert	Soldier	Thomas Newburgh's Foot Company
Foster	John	Soldier	Sir John Vaughan's Foot Company
Foster	Richard	Soldier	Jasper Hartwell's Foot Company
Foster	Edward	Soldier	Tristram Berisford's Foot Company
Fowler	John	Corporal	Henry Finch's Foot Company
Foxley	Anthony	Soldier	Jasper Hartwell's Foot Company
Freeman	William	Soldier	Sir John Vaughan's Foot Company
Fren	John	Soldier	Tristram Berisford's Foot Company
Gaje	Thomas	Soldier	Henry Osborne's Foot Company
Galbraith	Martin	Soldier	Henry Finch's Foot Company
Galloher	John	Soldier	Tristram Berisford's Foot Company
Gamble	John	Soldier	Sir Thomas Staples' Foot Company
Gamble	John	Corporal	Henry Osborne's Foot Company
Gamble	Robert	Soldier	Henry Osborne's Foot Company
Gamble	William	Soldier	Henry Osborne's Foot Company
Gardner	Christopher	Soldier	Robert Thornton's Foot Company
Gardner	William	Soldier	Robert Thornton's Foot Company
Gates	John	Soldier	Henry Finch's Foot Company
Gelvery	Manus	Soldier	John Kilner's Foot Company

DEFENDERS OF LONDONDERRY, 1642

Surname	First Name	Rank	Company
Genions	ffra	Soldier	Sir John Vaughan's Foot Company
Geymes	John	Soldier	Sir John Vaughan's Foot Company
Gibson	Ringan	Soldier	Tristram Berisford's Foot Company
Giffine	John	Soldier	Henry Finch's Foot Company
Gifforde	George	Soldier	Henry Osborne's Foot Company
Gill	William	Soldier	Tristram Berisford's Foot Company
Gill	Henry	Soldier	Tristram Berisford's Foot Company
Gill	John	Soldier	Sir Thomas Staples' Foot Company
Giller	Robert	Soldier	Sir Thomas Staples' Foot Company
Gilliere	David	Soldier	Sir Thomas Staples' Foot Company
Gilsone	Robert	Soldier	Henry Osborne's Foot Company
Gimble	James	Soldier	Sir Thomas Staples' Foot Company
Godffrey	George	Drummer	Tristram Berisford's Foot Company
Goebreth	Humphrey	Soldier	Jasper Hartwell's Foot Company
Golterye	John	Soldier	John Kilner's Foot Company
Goltorye	Archibald	Soldier	John Kilner's Foot Company
Goodwin	Bryan	Soldier	Jasper Hartwell's Foot Company
Goose	Edward	Soldier	Henry Finch's Foot Company
Gore	James	Soldier	Robert Thornton's Foot Company
Gorman	John	Soldier	Sir Thomas Staples' Foot Company
Gotery	James	Soldier	John Kilner's Foot Company
Gottery	John	Soldier	John Kilner's Foot Company
Gottery	Samuell	Soldier	John Kilner's Foot Company
Graft	Francis	Soldier	Thomas Newburgh's Foot Company
Graham	Francis	Sergeant	Thomas Newburgh's Foot Company
Graye	Allex	Soldier	Tristram Berisford's Foot Company
Gredine	John	Soldier	Henry Osborne's Foot Company
Grene	Thomas	Soldier	Henry Finch's Foot Company
Greyme	Peter	Soldier	Robert Thornton's Foot Company
Griffin	Rice	Soldier	Sir John Vaughan's Foot Company
Griffin	William	Soldier	Sir John Vaughan's Foot Company
Griffin	Edward	Soldier	Thomas Newburgh's Foot Company
Griffin	Sallamon	Soldier	Sir Thomas Staples' Foot Company
Griffith	Ewin	Soldier	Tristram Berisford's Foot Company
Grodye	Manus	Soldier	Sir Thomas Staples' Foot Company
Groertye	Donell	Soldier	Sir Thomas Staples' Foot Company
Grosvenor	Richard	Corporal	Jasper Hartwell's Foot Company
Grymes	William	Soldier	Sir John Vaughan's Foot Company
Grymes	Richard	Soldier	Sir John Vaughan's Foot Company
Grymes	Daniell	Soldier	Sir John Vaughan's Foot Company
Guine	Elis	Sergeant	Tristram Berisford's Foot Company
Guthrye	Thomas	Soldier	Thomas Newburgh's Foot Company
Gyles	John	Soldier	Sir John Vaughan's Foot Company
Haire	John	Corporal	John Kilner's Foot Company
Haires	William	Soldier	Henry Osborne's Foot Company
Halton	Richard	Soldier	Sir John Vaughan's Foot Company
Hamilton	Andre	Corporal	Henry Finch's Foot Company
Hamilton	John	Soldier	Sir Thomas Staples' Foot Company
Hamilton	William	Soldier	Henry Osborne's Foot Company
Hamilton	William	Soldier	Henry Osborne's Foot Company
Hamond	Andrew	Soldier	Sir John Vaughan's Foot Company
Hamond	Richard	Soldier	Robert Thornton's Foot Company
Hanah	Thomas	Soldier	Sir Thomas Staples' Foot Company
Handlinge	William	Soldier	Henry Finch's Foot Company

DEFENDERS OF LONDONDERRY, 1642

Surname	First Name	Rank	Company
Hannock	Alford	Soldier	Sir John Vaughan's Foot Company
Harison	Thomas	Soldier	Thomas Newburgh's Foot Company
Harison	John	Soldier	Robert Thornton's Foot Company
Harmond	Thomas	Soldier	Tristram Berisford's Foot Company
Haroll	Thomas	Soldier	Robert Thornton's Foot Company
Harper	Allex	Soldier	Henry Osborne's Foot Company
Harrye	John	Soldier	Sir Thomas Staples' Foot Company
Hart	Eustace	Soldier	Robert Thornton's Foot Company
Hartt	Thomas	Soldier	Robert Thornton's Foot Company
Hartt	Merick	Soldier	Robert Thornton's Foot Company
Hartwell	Jasper	Captain	Jasper Hartwell's Foot Company
Hartwell	Richard	Lieutenant	Jasper Hartwell's Foot Company
Harvye	John	Soldier	Sir Thomas Staples' Foot Company
Harwod	John	Soldier	Sir Thomas Staples' Foot Company
Hasellwood	Robert	Soldier	Jasper Hartwell's Foot Company
Haugten	Charles	Soldier	Tristram Berisford's Foot Company
Hawkes	John	Soldier	Robert Thornton's Foot Company
Hayden	Tristam	Soldier	Tristram Berisford's Foot Company
Haye	John	Soldier	Sir Thomas Staples' Foot Company
Haye	John	Soldier	Sir Thomas Staples' Foot Company
Hea	Nicolas	Soldier	Sir Thomas Staples' Foot Company
Heard	Steephen	Corporal	Sir John Vaughan's Foot Company
Heath	John	Corporal	Thomas Newburgh's Foot Company
Heatlye	John	Soldier	Robert Thornton's Foot Company
Heaton	John	Sergeant	Robert Thornton's Foot Company
Heaton	John	Soldier	Robert Thornton's Foot Company
Hender	Thomas	Soldier	Henry Finch's Foot Company
Hender	Peter	Soldier	Henry Finch's Foot Company
Henderson	John	Soldier	John Kilner's Foot Company
Henrick	John	Soldier	Sir Thomas Staples' Foot Company
Henrye	William	Soldier	John Kilner's Foot Company
Herd	Stephen	Soldier	Tristram Berisford's Foot Company
Herris	John	Soldier	John Kilner's Foot Company
Heye	John	Soldier	Henry Osborne's Foot Company
Heye	Andrew	Soldier	Henry Osborne's Foot Company
Hindman	James	Soldier	Henry Osborne's Foot Company
Hindman	William	Soldier	Henry Osborne's Foot Company
Holmes	Thomas	Soldier	Henry Osborne's Foot Company
Hoode	Archibald	Soldier	Henry Finch's Foot Company
Hopkins	John	Soldier	John Kilner's Foot Company
Houle	Anthony	Soldier	Robert Thornton's Foot Company
Howard	Francis	Soldier	Thomas Newburgh's Foot Company
Howe	Richard	Soldier	Thomas Newburgh's Foot Company
Howell	Christopher	Soldier	Henry Finch's Foot Company
Hoyle	John	Soldier	Tristram Berisford's Foot Company
Hucheson	Thomas	Soldier	Tristram Berisford's Foot Company
Hudcen	Edward	Soldier	Sir Thomas Staples' Foot Company
Hughes	Owin	Drummer	Sir John Vaughan's Foot Company
Hullye	Robert	Soldier	Henry Finch's Foot Company
Hullye	Edward	Soldier	Henry Finch's Foot Company
Hullye	John	Soldier	Henry Finch's Foot Company
Hunter	John	Soldier	Tristram Berisford's Foot Company
Hustone	James	Soldier	Henry Finch's Foot Company
Hustone	William	Soldier	Sir Thomas Staples' Foot Company

DEFENDERS OF LONDONDERRY, 1642

Surname	First Name	Rank	Company
Hustone	John	Soldier	John Kilner's Foot Company
Hutson	John	Soldier	Sir Thomas Staples' Foot Company
Jackson	John	Soldier	Sir John Vaughan's Foot Company
Jackson	Hercules	Soldier	Robert Thornton's Foot Company
Jameson	Dunkan	Soldier	Tristram Berisford's Foot Company
Jamison	John	Soldier	Thomas Newburgh's Foot Company
Jenkin	Euan	Soldier	John Kilner's Foot Company
Jennins	John	Soldier	Thomas Newburgh's Foot Company
Johnson	George	Soldier	Sir John Vaughan's Foot Company
Johnson	George	Sergeant	Sir Thomas Staples' Foot Company
Johnson	Andrew	Soldier	Sir Thomas Staples' Foot Company
Johnson	George	Soldier	Sir Thomas Staples' Foot Company
Johnson	William	Soldier	Tristram Berisford's Foot Company
Johnson	Allex	Soldier	Henry Osborne's Foot Company
Johnstone	Archibald	Soldier	Henry Osborne's Foot Company
Kadwallader	David	Soldier	Sir John Vaughan's Foot Company
Keile	Laws	Soldier	Thomas Newburgh's Foot Company
Keile	William	Soldier	Tristram Berisford's Foot Company
Kellye	John	Soldier	Henry Finch's Foot Company
Kellye	James	Soldier	Henry Osborne's Foot Company
Kellye	William	Soldier	Henry Osborne's Foot Company
Kenedye	John	Soldier	Henry Finch's Foot Company
Kennedy	John	Soldier	Jasper Hartwell's Foot Company
Kenwood	Phillips	Soldier	Jasper Hartwell's Foot Company
Kerbye	Robert	Soldier	Henry Finch's Foot Company
Kerr	James	Soldier	Henry Osborne's Foot Company
Ketlebye	George	Soldier	Sir Thomas Staples' Foot Company
Keyle	John	Soldier	Sir John Vaughan's Foot Company
Kilner	John	Captain	John Kilner's Foot Company
King	Thomas	Soldier	Sir John Vaughan's Foot Company
Kinge	William	Soldier	Tristram Berisford's Foot Company
Kinge	Mathew	Soldier	John Kilner's Foot Company
Kinge	Robert	Soldier	John Kilner's Foot Company
Kinkaide	Niniam	Soldier	Henry Osborne's Foot Company
Kitwallader	Hugh	Soldier	Sir John Vaughan's Foot Company
Knelan	John	Soldier	Sir Thomas Staples' Foot Company
Kneland	William	Soldier	Sir Thomas Staples' Foot Company
Knocks	James	Soldier	Sir John Vaughan's Foot Company
Knowles	Edward	Soldier	Sir Thomas Staples' Foot Company
Knowles	John	Soldier	Sir Thomas Staples' Foot Company
Knowles	Felix	Soldier	Sir Thomas Staples' Foot Company
Knox	Henry	Soldier	Henry Osborne's Foot Company
Knox	Thomas	Soldier	Henry Osborne's Foot Company
Knt	John	Soldier	Sir Thomas Staples' Foot Company
Labe	James	Soldier	Sir Thomas Staples' Foot Company
Lach?	Thomas	Soldier	Sir Thomas Staples' Foot Company
Lamkin	Hugh	Drummer	Jasper Hartwell's Foot Company
Lane	Nicolas	Lieutenant	Robert Thornton's Foot Company
Langforde	John	Soldier	Henry Osborne's Foot Company
Langmore	John	Soldier	Henry Finch's Foot Company
Langton	Charles	Soldier	Henry Finch's Foot Company
Langton	Henry	Drummer	Sir Thomas Staples' Foot Company
Laulin	Manus	Soldier	Sir Thomas Staples' Foot Company
Lawe	Thomas	Corporal	Tristram Berisford's Foot Company

DEFENDERS OF LONDONDERRY, 1642

Surname	First Name	Rank	Company
Lawrence	John	Soldier	Thomas Newburgh's Foot Company
Lawson	Christopher	Soldier	Robert Thornton's Foot Company
Lawton	William	Coporal	Robert Thornton's Foot Company
Lea	Thomas	Soldier	Sir John Vaughan's Foot Company
Lea	Peter	Soldier	Sir John Vaughan's Foot Company
Lee	Richard	Soldier	Tristram Berisford's Foot Company
Lenen	George	Soldier	Henry Osborne's Foot Company
Lenry	Thomas	Soldier	Henry Osborne's Foot Company
Lewis	Symon	Soldier	Sir John Vaughan's Foot Company
Lewis	Thomas	Soldier	Robert Thornton's Foot Company
Lewis	John	Soldier	John Kilner's Foot Company
Lewis	Edmond	Soldier	John Kilner's Foot Company
Lindsey	James	Soldier	John Kilner's Foot Company
Lindseye	Mathew	Soldier	Henry Finch's Foot Company
Linne	John	Soldier	Henry Osborne's Foot Company
Logan	John	Soldier	Henry Osborne's Foot Company
Lone	John	Sergeant	Henry Osborne's Foot Company
Long	John	Soldier	Sir John Vaughan's Foot Company
Longe	James	Soldier	Robert Thornton's Foot Company
Longe	John	Soldier	Henry Osborne's Foot Company
Longe	James	Soldier	Henry Osborne's Foot Company
Longe	William	Soldier	Henry Osborne's Foot Company
Lyn	William	Soldier	Sir John Vaughan's Foot Company
Lyn	John	Soldier	Sir John Vaughan's Foot Company
Macbellane	James	Soldier	Sir Thomas Staples' Foot Company
Mack	James	Soldier	Jasper Hartwell's Foot Company
Mack	William	Soldier	John Kilner's Foot Company
Mackillney	John	Soldier	Jasper Hartwell's Foot Company
Mackrery	John	Soldier	Jasper Hartwell's Foot Company
Mackrery	James	Soldier	Jasper Hartwell's Foot Company
Mackrone	Andrew	Soldier	Jasper Hartwell's Foot Company
Maconahye	Allex	Soldier	John Kilner's Foot Company
Macowell	Allan	Soldier	Sir Thomas Staples' Foot Company
Mader	William	Soldier	Tristram Berisford's Foot Company
Maderell	John	Soldier	Henry Finch's Foot Company
Madernell	Andrew	Soldier	Henry Finch's Foot Company
Madley	John	Soldier	Jasper Hartwell's Foot Company
Madox	Peter	Soldier	Henry Finch's Foot Company
Madox	George	Soldier	Henry Finch's Foot Company
Magee	John	Soldier	Henry Finch's Foot Company
Magee	William	Soldier	Tristram Berisford's Foot Company
Magee	Allex	Soldier	Robert Thornton's Foot Company
Magowen	John	Soldier	Henry Finch's Foot Company
Magowne	Daniel	Soldier	Jasper Hartwell's Foot Company
Magowne	Fergus	Soldier	Sir Thomas Staples' Foot Company
Maior	James	Soldier	Henry Finch's Foot Company
Makaye	Daniell	Drummer	Thomas Newburgh's Foot Company
Makee	David	Soldier	Sir Thomas Staples' Foot Company
Makennis	Allex	Soldier	Tristram Berisford's Foot Company
Makeye	Hugh	Soldier	Tristram Berisford's Foot Company
Makim	Robert	Soldier	Sir Thomas Staples' Foot Company
Making	John	Corporal	Henry Osborne's Foot Company
Maklane	Thomas	Soldier	Robert Thornton's Foot Company
Malcollum	Gill	Soldier	Sir Thomas Staples' Foot Company

DEFENDERS OF LONDONDERRY, 1642

Surname	First Name	Rank	Company
Marsh	James	Soldier	Jasper Hartwell's Foot Company
Marshall	Hugh	Soldier	Tristram Berisford's Foot Company
Marshall	William	Soldier	John Kilner's Foot Company
Martiall	Allex	Soldier	Sir Thomas Staples' Foot Company
Martin	John	Soldier	John Kilner's Foot Company
Martine	John	Soldier	Thomas Newburgh's Foot Company
Masters	Ralph	Soldier	Robert Thornton's Foot Company
Matginsey	John	Soldier	Jasper Hartwell's Foot Company
Mathews	John	Soldier	Henry Finch's Foot Company
Matire	Patrick	Soldier	Henry Finch's Foot Company
Maxwell	Robert	Soldier	Tristram Berisford's Foot Company
McArtan	Con	Soldier	Robert Thornton's Foot Company
McBoyle	William	Soldier	John Kilner's Foot Company
McCallen	Teage	Soldier	Robert Thornton's Foot Company
McCavere	Owin	Soldier	Sir John Vaughan's Foot Company
McCawley	John	Soldier	Thomas Newburgh's Foot Company
Mcffarlan	Thomas	Soldier	Henry Osborne's Foot Company
Mcffarlan	Daniel	Soldier	John Kilner's Foot Company
McGill	John	Soldier	Sir John Vaughan's Foot Company
McGilligan	Cormack	Soldier	Sir John Vaughan's Foot Company
McIldue	Walter	Soldier	Sir Thomas Staples' Foot Company
McKenlen	John	Soldier	Tristram Berisford's Foot Company
McKilcome	Simon	Soldier	Henry Finch's Foot Company
McKilcrone	Rory	Soldier	Henry Osborne's Foot Company
McKiltire	Robert	Soldier	Henry Finch's Foot Company
McKiltire	Gilbert	Soldier	Henry Finch's Foot Company
McKiltire	John	Soldier	Henry Finch's Foot Company
McKiltire	Phillip	Soldier	Henry Finch's Foot Company
McLanlin	William	Soldier	Robert Thornton's Foot Company
McLochin	Turloch	Soldier	Henry Finch's Foot Company
McLocklin	Donohy	Soldier	Henry Finch's Foot Company
McRuden	Neale	Soldier	Robert Thornton's Foot Company
McShaden	Gilchrist	Soldier	Robert Thornton's Foot Company
McWaller	Brise	Soldier	Henry Osborne's Foot Company
McWilly	John	Soldier	John Kilner's Foot Company
Meads	Tobias	Soldier	Tristram Berisford's Foot Company
Medcalfe	William	Sergeant	Sir John Vaughan's Foot Company
Medcalfe	James	Soldier	Sir John Vaughan's Foot Company
Mell	John	Soldier	John Kilner's Foot Company
Metland	Andrew	Soldier	Robert Thornton's Foot Company
Michell	William	Soldier	Henry Finch's Foot Company
Michell	Walter	Soldier	Sir Thomas Staples' Foot Company
Michell	Mungoe	Soldier	Sir Thomas Staples' Foot Company
Michell	John	Soldier	Robert Thornton's Foot Company
Miller	John	Soldier	Thomas Newburgh's Foot Company
Milles	John	Soldier	John Kilner's Foot Company
Moldrage	John	Drummer	Henry Finch's Foot Company
Mollchellin	Mellin	Soldier	Tristram Berisford's Foot Company
Moncreife	Thomas	Lieutenant	Henry Osborne's Foot Company
Moncrieff	John	Soldier	Robert Thornton's Foot Company
Moore	Edward	Corporal	Sir Thomas Staples' Foot Company
Moore	William	Soldier	Sir Thomas Staples' Foot Company
Moore	Richard	Soldier	Tristram Berisford's Foot Company
Moore	Thomas	Soldier	Robert Thornton's Foot Company

DEFENDERS OF LONDONDERRY, 1642

Surname	First Name	Rank	Company
More	William	Soldier	Thomas Newburgh's Foot Company
More	John	Soldier	Thomas Newburgh's Foot Company
More	John	Drummer	John Kilner's Foot Company
More	Robert	Soldier	John Kilner's Foot Company
Morges	James	Soldier	Henry Osborne's Foot Company
Morison	Hugh	Soldier	Sir John Vaughan's Foot Company
Morison	Robert	Soldier	Henry Finch's Foot Company
Morison	James	Soldier	Tristram Berisford's Foot Company
Morison	John	Soldier	John Kilner's Foot Company
Morthwan	Ada	Soldier	Henry Finch's Foot Company
Moules	William	Soldier	Henry Osborne's Foot Company
Mount	Robert	Soldier	Jasper Hartwell's Foot Company
Mullan	William	Soldier	John Kilner's Foot Company
Mulloh	Hugh	Soldier	Thomas Newburgh's Foot Company
Murdock	William	Soldier	Robert Thornton's Foot Company
Murphett	Christopher	Soldier	Sir Thomas Staples' Foot Company
Naughtley	John	Soldier	Jasper Hartwell's Foot Company
Nevill	Henry	Sergeant	Jasper Hartwell's Foot Company
Newburgh	Thomas	Captain	Thomas Newburgh's Foot Company
Newburgh	Thomas	Ensign	Thomas Newburgh's Foot Company
Newburgh	Thomas	Soldier	Thomas Newburgh's Foot Company
Newburgh	Arthur	Soldier	Thomas Newburgh's Foot Company
Newcomb	Thomas	Soldier	Thomas Newburgh's Foot Company
Nicollson	Henry	Ensign	Sir Thomas Staples' Foot Company
Nillen	Thomas	Soldier	Tristram Berisford's Foot Company
Nixon	James	Soldier	Sir Thomas Staples' Foot Company
Norde	John	Soldier	Henry Finch's Foot Company
Norman	Richard	Soldier	Sir John Vaughan's Foot Company
Nottrice	William	Soldier	Jasper Hartwell's Foot Company
Nutt	John	Soldier	John Kilner's Foot Company
Nutt	Robert	Soldier	John Kilner's Foot Company
O'Bryne	Donoghy	Soldier	Sir John Vaughan's Foot Company
O'Cahan	George	Soldier	Robert Thornton's Foot Company
O'Cane	Hugh	Soldier	John Kilner's Foot Company
O'Dermont	Pheleney	Soldier	John Kilner's Foot Company
O'Dermont	John	Soldier	John Kilner's Foot Company
O'Derry	Hanry	Soldier	Henry Osborne's Foot Company
O'Doherty	Hugh	Soldier	Robert Thornton's Foot Company
O'Dohertye	Owen	Soldier	Henry Finch's Foot Company
O'Dowe	Dermont	Soldier	John Kilner's Foot Company
O'Drey	Philomy	Soldier	Sir John Vaughan's Foot Company
O'Durrye	Cormack	Soldier	Sir Thomas Staples' Foot Company
O'Galloher	James	Soldier	Henry Finch's Foot Company
O'Galloher	Owen	Soldier	Henry Finch's Foot Company
O'Galloher	Daniel	Soldier	Sir Thomas Staples' Foot Company
Ogle	William	Soldier	Tristram Berisford's Foot Company
O'Hagarty	Edmund	Soldier	Robert Thornton's Foot Company
O'Harkan	Nece	Soldier	Tristram Berisford's Foot Company
O'Haveland	Owen	Soldier	Tristram Berisford's Foot Company
O'Kean	Darby	Soldier	Henry Finch's Foot Company
O'Kine	John	Soldier	Henry Osborne's Foot Company
O'Lancarie	Gilbert	Soldier	Henry Osborne's Foot Company
O'Lasheye	John	Soldier	Henry Osborne's Foot Company
O'Lashye	Edmond	Soldier	Henry Osborne's Foot Company

DEFENDERS OF LONDONDERRY, 1642

Surname	First Name	Rank	Company
O'Laulin	Edmond	Soldier	John Kilner's Foot Company
O'Leckye	Robert	Soldier	Henry Osborne's Foot Company
O'Lenerick	Dermont	Soldier	Tristram Berisford's Foot Company
O'Line	Rory	Soldier	John Kilner's Foot Company
O'Linshanan	William	Soldier	Henry Finch's Foot Company
O'Mullan	Darby	Soldier	Henry Finch's Foot Company
O'Mullan	James	Soldier	Robert Thornton's Foot Company
O'Qustion	Hugh	Soldier	Sir Thomas Staples' Foot Company
O'Reall	Owen	Soldier	Robert Thornton's Foot Company
Orr	John	Soldier	Sir Thomas Staples' Foot Company
Orr	John	Soldier	Tristram Berisford's Foot Company
Orr	William	Soldier	John Kilner's Foot Company
O'Rylie	Hugh	Soldier	Sir John Vaughan's Foot Company
Osborne	Henry	Soldier	Sir John Vaughan's Foot Company
Osborne	Henry	Captain	Henry Osborne's Foot Company
Osborne	Henry	Soldier	Henry Osborne's Foot Company
Osborne	George	Soldier	Henry Osborne's Foot Company
O'Sheale	Turloh	Soldier	John Kilner's Foot Company
O'Shene	Owen	Soldier	Tristram Berisford's Foot Company
O'Shenkye	Art	Soldier	Sir Thomas Staples' Foot Company
Owins	Robert	Soldier	Jasper Hartwell's Foot Company
Paine	David	Drummer	Robert Thornton's Foot Company
Palmer	Edward	Soldier	Robert Thornton's Foot Company
Parke	Thomas	Soldier	Henry Finch's Foot Company
Parker	Allen	Soldier	Henry Osborne's Foot Company
Parkes	Robert	Soldier	Robert Thornton's Foot Company
Parks	Robert	Soldier	Tristram Berisford's Foot Company
Parsons	Gilbert	Soldier	Sir John Vaughan's Foot Company
Parsons	John	Corporal	Tristram Berisford's Foot Company
Pasley	John	Soldier	Sir John Vaughan's Foot Company
Paterson	Robert	Soldier	Henry Finch's Foot Company
Paterson	John	Soldier	Henry Osborne's Foot Company
Paterson	Allex	Soldier	John Kilner's Foot Company
Paterson	William	Soldier	John Kilner's Foot Company
Paterson	John	Soldier	John Kilner's Foot Company
Patshall	William	Lieutenant	Sir John Vaughan's Foot Company
Patshall	William	Soldier	Sir John Vaughan's Foot Company
Patson	Mathew	Soldier	Robert Thornton's Foot Company
Paty	Jame	Soldier	Sir John Vaughan's Foot Company
Patyn	John	Soldier	Jasper Hartwell's Foot Company
Pearman	Edward	Soldier	Robert Thornton's Foot Company
Peirce	Robert	Corporal	Robert Thornton's Foot Company
Peirmon	John	Soldier	Henry Finch's Foot Company
Penman	John	Soldier	John Kilner's Foot Company
Percee	James	Soldier	Sir Thomas Staples' Foot Company
Perry	Thomas	Soldier	Tristram Berisford's Foot Company
Pett	Arthur	Soldier	Henry Osborne's Foot Company
Phetis	Neale	Soldier	Tristram Berisford's Foot Company
Pigott	Hugh	Soldier	Thomas Newburgh's Foot Company
Piott	Richard	Sergeant	Robert Thornton's Foot Company
Pits	Nathaniell	Soldier	Sir John Vaughan's Foot Company
Pitts	Richard	Soldier	Sir John Vaughan's Foot Company
Plott	Thomas	Drummer	Sir John Vaughan's Foot Company
Plunkett	John	Corporal	Robert Thornton's Foot Company

DEFENDERS OF LONDONDERRY, 1642

Surname	First Name	Rank	Company
Poage	Robert	Soldier	Thomas Newburgh's Foot Company
Poake	William	Soldier	John Kilner's Foot Company
Poake	James	Soldier	John Kilner's Foot Company
Poge	Thomas	Soldier	Thomas Newburgh's Foot Company
Poge	William	Soldier	Sir Thomas Staples' Foot Company
Potts	Francis	Soldier	Jasper Hartwell's Foot Company
Prigeon	Henry	Corporal	Sir John Vaughan's Foot Company
Prigeon	Richard	Soldier	Sir John Vaughan's Foot Company
Pryce	Symond	Soldier	Sir John Vaughan's Foot Company
Purdie	John	Soldier	Thomas Newburgh's Foot Company
Pustye	Richard	Soldier	Tristram Berisford's Foot Company
Pustye	William	Soldier	Tristram Berisford's Foot Company
Qugge	John	Soldier	Robert Thornton's Foot Company
Quigleye	Edward	Soldier	Thomas Newburgh's Foot Company
Quigly	Roger	Soldier	Thomas Newburgh's Foot Company
Quinton	Allex	Soldier	Thomas Newburgh's Foot Company
Rabb	James	Soldier	Henry Finch's Foot Company
Raimer	James	Soldier	John Kilner's Foot Company
Raimonde	Stephen	Soldier	Tristram Berisford's Foot Company
Ramese	Thomas	Soldier	John Kilner's Foot Company
Ramir	Alexander	Soldier	John Kilner's Foot Company
Ramseye	Thomas	Soldier	Henry Osborne's Foot Company
Ramseye	Gowen	Soldier	Henry Osborne's Foot Company
Randle	John	Soldier	Sir Thomas Staples' Foot Company
Randle	James	Soldier	Sir Thomas Staples' Foot Company
Randle	Robert	Soldier	Sir Thomas Staples' Foot Company
Ranken	John	Soldier	Tristram Berisford's Foot Company
Ranken	Philip	Soldier	Henry Osborne's Foot Company
Rankine	Thomas	Soldier	Henry Finch's Foot Company
Ranolds	James	Soldier	Robert Thornton's Foot Company
Raven	Richard	Corporal	Sir Thomas Staples' Foot Company
Raye	William	Soldier	Thomas Newburgh's Foot Company
Raysdale	John	Soldier	Thomas Newburgh's Foot Company
Rea	William	Drummer	Henry Finch's Foot Company
Read	John	Soldier	Sir John Vaughan's Foot Company
Reade	Wall	Soldier	Thomas Newburgh's Foot Company
Reade	Robert	Soldier	Sir Thomas Staples' Foot Company
Reade	John	Soldier	Robert Thornton's Foot Company
Reddall	Archibald	Soldier	Sir John Vaughan's Foot Company
Reynolds	Thomas	Soldier	Sir John Vaughan's Foot Company
Richarde	Patrick	Soldier	Henry Osborne's Foot Company
Richards	William ap	Soldier	Tristram Berisford's Foot Company
Richerson	Tuistram	Soldier	Henry Osborne's Foot Company
Richman	Nicholas	Soldier	Sir John Vaughan's Foot Company
Ridley	Richard	Sergeant	Thomas Newburgh's Foot Company
Rile	John	Soldier	Henry Osborne's Foot Company
Rinde	John	Soldier	Robert Thornton's Foot Company
Ripley	Mathew	Soldier	Sir John Vaughan's Foot Company
Roback	John	Soldier	Robert Thornton's Foot Company
Robb	David	Soldier	Sir Thomas Staples' Foot Company
Roberts	William	Soldier	Robert Thornton's Foot Company
Robinson	Hugh	Soldier	Sir John Vaughan's Foot Company
Robinson	James	Soldier	Henry Finch's Foot Company
Robinson	John	Soldier	Henry Finch's Foot Company

DEFENDERS OF LONDONDERRY, 1642

Surname	First Name	Rank	Company
Robinson	George	Soldier	Thomas Newburgh's Foot Company
Robinson	Hugh	Soldier	Thomas Newburgh's Foot Company
Robinson	Leonard	Soldier	Thomas Newburgh's Foot Company
Robinson	William	Soldier	Robert Thornton's Foot Company
Robinson	Michaell	Soldier	John Kilner's Foot Company
Robinson	Gowen	Soldier	John Kilner's Foot Company
Robinson	Robert	Soldier	John Kilner's Foot Company
Robison	John	Soldier	Tristram Berisford's Foot Company
Robison	Thomas	Soldier	Robert Thornton's Foot Company
Roes	John	Soldier	Sir Thomas Staples' Foot Company
Rogers	Walter	Soldier	Sir John Vaughan's Foot Company
Rogers	Allen	Soldier	John Kilner's Foot Company
Rootelidge	Francis	Solder	Jasper Hartwell's Foot Company
Rose	John	Soldier	Jasper Hartwell's Foot Company
Ross	Antony	Soldier	John Kilner's Foot Company
Ross	Brian	Soldier	John Kilner's Foot Company
Rosse	Laughlin	Soldier	Sir John Vaughan's Foot Company
Rudd	John	Soldier	John Kilner's Foot Company
Ruddall	Andrew	Soldier	John Kilner's Foot Company
Rudden	John	Soldier	Tristram Berisford's Foot Company
Rude	William	Soldier	Jasper Hartwell's Foot Company
Rudle	John	Soldier	John Kilner's Foot Company
Rue	Walter	Corporal	Tristram Berisford's Foot Company
Russell	John	Soldier	Jasper Hartwell's Foot Company
Sandelam	Gilbert	Soldier	Tristram Berisford's Foot Company
Sanders	George	Soldier	Sir John Vaughan's Foot Company
Sanders	Thomas	Soldier	Tristram Berisford's Foot Company
Savage	William	Soldier	Thomas Newburgh's Foot Company
Scot	Alex	Soldier	John Kilner's Foot Company
Scott	David	Soldier	Sir John Vaughan's Foot Company
Scott	Henry	Soldier	Sir John Vaughan's Foot Company
Scott	Thomas	Soldier	Henry Osborne's Foot Company
Scott	John	Soldier	Henry Osborne's Foot Company
Seaton	William	Soldier	Thomas Newburgh's Foot Company
Sharpe	Francis	Corporal	Sir Thomas Staples' Foot Company
Sharpe	Grabriell	Soldier	Tristram Berisford's Foot Company
Sharpe	Nathaniell	Soldier	Henry Osborne's Foot Company
Shaw	John	Soldier	Thomas Newburgh's Foot Company
Sherley	John	Soldier	Jasper Hartwell's Foot Company
Shevington	Edward	Drummer	Sir John Vaughan's Foot Company
Shirlock	Peter	Soldier	Sir John Vaughan's Foot Company
Shursby	John	Soldier	Sir John Vaughan's Foot Company
Sill	John	Soldier	Sir John Vaughan's Foot Company
Simson	Andrew	Soldier	Thomas Newburgh's Foot Company
Simson	Robert	Soldier	Tristram Berisford's Foot Company
Simson	James	Soldier	Tristram Berisford's Foot Company
Skamon	John	Soldier	Robert Thornton's Foot Company
Skevington	Thomas	Soldier	Robert Thornton's Foot Company
Skiner	William	Soldier	Robert Thornton's Foot Company
Skipton	Thomas	Ensign	Robert Thornton's Foot Company
Slatter	William	Soldier	Tristram Berisford's Foot Company
Sloane	John	Sergeant	John Kilner's Foot Company
Smith	John	Sergeant	Sir John Vaughan's Foot Company
Smith	John	Corporal	Jasper Hartwell's Foot Company

DEFENDERS OF LONDONDERRY, 1642

Surname	First Name	Rank	Company
Smith	Gawen	Soldier	Jasper Hartwell's Foot Company
Smith	William	Soldier	Jasper Hartwell's Foot Company
Smith	John	Soldier	Henry Finch's Foot Company
Smith	William	Soldier	Henry Finch's Foot Company
Smith	James	Soldier	Henry Finch's Foot Company
Smith	Samuel	Soldier	Thomas Newburgh's Foot Company
Smith	Luan	Soldier	Thomas Newburgh's Foot Company
Smith	John	Soldier	Sir Thomas Staples' Foot Company
Smith	Thomas	Soldier	Sir Thomas Staples' Foot Company
Smith	William	Soldier	Tristram Berisford's Foot Company
Smith	David	Soldier	Tristram Berisford's Foot Company
Smith	Richard	Soldier	Robert Thornton's Foot Company
Smith	Gabriell	Soldier	Henry Osborne's Foot Company
Smith	George	Soldier	Henry Osborne's Foot Company
Smith	John	Soldier	Henry Osborne's Foot Company
Smith	Ellis	Soldier	John Kilner's Foot Company
Smith	Edward	Soldier	John Kilner's Foot Company
Sparks	Thomas	Soldier	Tristram Berisford's Foot Company
Spencer	Lowe	Soldier	Thomas Newburgh's Foot Company
Springhan	William	Soldier	Tristram Berisford's Foot Company
Stanley	Rowland	Soldier	Jasper Hartwell's Foot Company
Stansby	Thomas	Soldier	Tristram Berisford's Foot Company
Staples	Sir Thomas	Captain	Sir Thomas Staples' Foot Company
Staples	Allexander	Lieutenant	Sir Thomas Staples' Foot Company
Staples	Babtist	Soldier	Sir Thomas Staples' Foot Company
Staples	Robert	Soldier	Sir Thomas Staples' Foot Company
Steile	Hugh	Soldier	Thomas Newburgh's Foot Company
Steile	James	Soldier	Henry Osborne's Foot Company
Stenson	David	Soldier	Henry Osborne's Foot Company
Stenson	John	Soldier	Henry Osborne's Foot Company
Stenson	Robert	Soldier	Henry Osborne's Foot Company
Sterlinge	James	Soldier	John Kilner's Foot Company
Sterlinge	William	Soldier	John Kilner's Foot Company
Stevenson	Edward	Soldier	Sir John Vaughan's Foot Company
Stevson	Thomas	Soldier	John Kilner's Foot Company
Steward	John	Soldier	Jasper Hartwell's Foot Company
Stewart	Thomas	Soldier	Robert Thornton's Foot Company
Stewart	John	Soldier	Robert Thornton's Foot Company
Stewart	Robert	Soldier	Robert Thornton's Foot Company
Stewart	Lecky	Drummer	Henry Osborne's Foot Company
Stewart	William	Drummer	Henry Osborne's Foot Company
Stewart	Robert	Soldier	Henry Osborne's Foot Company
Stewart	John	Soldier	John Kilner's Foot Company
Stillye	Adam	Soldier	Sir Thomas Staples' Foot Company
Stinson	John	Soldier	Jasper Hartwell's Foot Company
Stinson	John	Soldier	Thomas Newburgh's Foot Company
Stotesbury	Henry	Drummer	Tristram Berisford's Foot Company
Stotsburye	William	Soldier	Tristram Berisford's Foot Company
Swan	John	Soldier	Jasper Hartwell's Foot Company
Swan	Edward	Corporal	John Kilner's Foot Company
Swyne	Daniel	Soldier	Jasper Hartwell's Foot Company
Tackett	John	Soldier	Sir Thomas Staples' Foot Company
Taire	John	Soldier	Henry Osborne's Foot Company
Tallen	Henry	Soldier	Henry Finch's Foot Company

DEFENDERS OF LONDONDERRY, 1642

Surname	First Name	Rank	Company
Tare	John	Soldier	Thomas Newburgh's Foot Company
Tathe	William	Corporal	Jasper Hartwell's Foot Company
Taylor	Thomas	Soldier	Tristram Berisford's Foot Company
Templetinton	James	Soldier	John Kilner's Foot Company
Terre	Daniel	Soldier	Tristram Berisford's Foot Company
Terry	Henry	Corporal	Thomas Newburgh's Foot Company
Thomas	Miles	Soldier	Tristram Berisford's Foot Company
Thornton	Robert	Captain	Robert Thornton's Foot Company
Thornton	Richard	Soldier	Robert Thornton's Foot Company
Thornton	Thomas	Soldier	Robert Thornton's Foot Company
Tompson	John	Soldier	Jasper Hartwell's Foot Company
Tomson	Abraham	Soldier	Sir John Vaughan's Foot Company
Tomson	Robert	Soldier	Sir Thomas Staples' Foot Company
Tomson	Mathew	Soldier	Robert Thornton's Foot Company
Tomson	David	Soldier	Robert Thornton's Foot Company
Tomson	George	Ensign	Henry Osborne's Foot Company
Tomson	William	Soldier	Henry Osborne's Foot Company
Tomson	Johan	Soldier	John Kilner's Foot Company
Topine	John	Soldier	Henry Finch's Foot Company
Towers	John	Soldier	John Kilner's Foot Company
Townsend	Edward	Soldier	Robert Thornton's Foot Company
Toyden	Daniell	Soldier	Tristram Berisford's Foot Company
Trape	William	Soldier	Tristram Berisford's Foot Company
Trevor	Robert	Soldier	Sir John Vaughan's Foot Company
Turbat	Allin	Soldier	Sir Thomas Staples' Foot Company
Turbett	William	Soldier	Henry Finch's Foot Company
Turbett	Mathew	Soldier	Robert Thornton's Foot Company
Turbett	John	Soldier	Robert Thornton's Foot Company
Turbett	Hugh	Soldier	Robert Thornton's Foot Company
Turbot	John	Soldier	Sir John Vaughan's Foot Company
Turner	William	Soldier	Tristram Berisford's Foot Company
Uinson	Allex	Soldier	Henry Osborne's Foot Company
Valaise	William	Soldier	Henry Osborne's Foot Company
Vaughan	Sir John	Captain	Sir John Vaughan's Foot Company
Veasie	James	Soldier	Sir John Vaughan's Foot Company
Walker	Finley	Soldier	Sir Thomas Staples' Foot Company
Walker	Allen	Soldier	Tristram Berisford's Foot Company
Wall	Richard	Soldier	Tristram Berisford's Foot Company
Wallace	James	Soldier	Sir John Vaughan's Foot Company
Wallace	John	Soldier	Robert Thornton's Foot Company
Wallace	Thomas	Soldier	Robert Thornton's Foot Company
Walters	Cane	Soldier	Henry Finch's Foot Company
Warren	Edward	Soldier	Sir John Vaughan's Foot Company
Warren	William	Soldier	Sir John Vaughan's Foot Company
Wats	James	Soldier	Henry Finch's Foot Company
Wats	Thomas	Soldier	Henry Finch's Foot Company
Watt	Robert	Soldier	Jasper Hartwell's Foot Company
Wayneman	Richard	Soldier	Jasper Hartwell's Foot Company
Webb	Richard	Drummer	Sir Thomas Staples' Foot Company
Webb	Henry	Soldier	Sir Thomas Staples' Foot Company
Weeks	Christopher	Soldier	Robert Thornton's Foot Company
Wescoinge	Marke	Sergeant	Henry Osborne's Foot Company
West	Joseph	Soldier	Robert Thornton's Foot Company
Westgate	John	Sergeant	Henry Finch's Foot Company

DEFENDERS OF LONDONDERRY, 1642

Surname	First Name	Rank	Company
Westock	Richard	Soldier	Tristram Berisford's Foot Company
Wharton	Robert	Soldier	Henry Finch's Foot Company
Wheadon	Anthony	Soldier	Sir John Vaughan's Foot Company
Wheadon	Thomas	Soldier	Sir John Vaughan's Foot Company
Wheadon	John	Soldier	Sir John Vaughan's Foot Company
White	John	Soldier	Thomas Newburgh's Foot Company
Wholmes	Thomas	Soldier	Sir John Vaughan's Foot Company
Wildrage	Thomas	Corporal	Henry Osborne's Foot Company
Wilkinson	John	Soldier	Sir John Vaughan's Foot Company
Willage	John	Soldier	Henry Osborne's Foot Company
William	John	Soldier	Robert Thornton's Foot Company
Williams	William	Soldier	Sir John Vaughan's Foot Company
Williams	Henry	Soldier	Sir John Vaughan's Foot Company
Williams	William	Soldier	Jasper Hartwell's Foot Company
Willington	Lawrence	Soldier	Robert Thornton's Foot Company
Willmson	William	Soldier	Sir Thomas Staples' Foot Company
Willson	James	Soldier	Henry Finch's Foot Company
Willson	Robert	Soldier	Thomas Newburgh's Foot Company
Willson	Lawrence	Soldier	Sir Thomas Staples' Foot Company
Willson	Robert	Soldier	Sir Thomas Staples' Foot Company
Willson	Andrew	Soldier	Robert Thornton's Foot Company
Willson	Mathew	Soldier	John Kilner's Foot Company
Willye	William	Soldier	Robert Thornton's Foot Company
Wilson	Robert	Soldier	Henry Finch's Foot Company
Wilson	John	Soldier	John Kilner's Foot Company
Witaker	Henry	Soldier	Henry Osborne's Foot Company
Wlms	Richard	Soldier	Tristram Berisford's Foot Company
Woods	George	Soldier	Thomas Newburgh's Foot Company
Wooll	George	Soldier	Robert Thornton's Foot Company
Wright	Patrick	Soldier	Henry Finch's Foot Company
Wright	Thomas	Soldier	Thomas Newburgh's Foot Company
Wright	Robert	Soldier	Robert Thornton's Foot Company
Wright	John	Soldier	John Kilner's Foot Company
Wurrall	Charles	Soldier	Sir Thomas Staples' Foot Company
Wurrall	Neah	Soldier	Sir Thomas Staples' Foot Company
Yarbar	William	Soldier	Robert Thornton's Foot Company
Younge	John	Soldier	Henry Finch's Foot Company
Younge	Allexander	Soldier	Sir Thomas Staples' Foot Company
Younge	Thomas	Soldier	Henry Osborne's Foot Company
	Gilbert	Soldier	Henry Finch's Foot Company
	John	Soldier	Henry Osborne's Foot Company

DEFENDERS OF IRELAND
DURING THE
WILLIAMITE WAR
OF 1689-1691

Young's ID	Surname	First Name	Residence	Remarks
1257	Abercromby	John	Drumcroe, Co. Fermanagh	Of an old Plantation family, active with defenders of Enniskillen
408	Abernethy	Lieutenant Josias	Moneymore, Co. Derry	Son of Rev John Abernethy, minister of Moneymore, who sent his wife and children to Derry for protection
467	Abram	Captain	Derry	
42	Acheson	Sir Nicholas	Market Hill, Co. Armagh	Great grandson of Archibald Acheson, the original grantee at the Plantation of the Market Hill estate. Created Earls of Gosford in 1806.
43	Acheson	Alexander	Tonihige, Co. Fermanagh	Son of Colonel William Acheson of Skea.
113	Adair	Sir Robert	Ballymena Castle, Co. Antrim	Grandson of Sir Robert Adair of Wigtownshire, Scotland who purchased the Ballymena estate from the Macquillans of the Route
114	Adair	Captain William	Ballymena, Co. Antrim	A brother or cousin of Sir Robert Adair (113)
115	Adair	Rev. Patrick	Carrickfergus, Co. Antrim	Presbyterian minister of Carrickfergus. Grandson of Sir Robert Adair (113)
116	Adair	Rev. William	Carrickfergus, Co. Antrim	Presbyterian minister
396	Adams	Captain Andrew	Strabane, Co. Tyrone	
397	Adams	David		
503	Adare	Thomas		Surgeon
1334	Addrington	Mathew	Co. Armagh	
985	Agnew	Patrick	Kilwaughter Castle, Larne, Co. Antrim	The Agnews of Lochnaw, near Stranraer, Wigtownshire, Scotland were settled at Kilwaughter prior to the Plantation
11	Aicken	Dr. Joseph	Derry	Author of 'Londeriados' poem detailing incidents and participants in the Siege. Published in Dublin in 1699.
1572	Airds	Mary		
738	Alcock	Adam		
1563	Aldrich	Francis	Enniskillen	Quartermaster in Wolseley's Horse
176	Alexander	Captain Andrew	Londonderry	Son of John Alexander who settled at Eredy, Co. Donegal in 1613. Andrew Alexander purchased Ballyclose estate, Limavady from Sir Thomas Phillips, and his eldest son, John purchased the estate of Gunsland (renamed Boomhall), overlooking the Foyle outside Derry.
1333	Allen	William	Co. Monaghan	
1574	Allen	Robert	Derry	
205	Ancketell	Mathew	Ancketell Grove, Co. Monaghan	Son of Oliver Ancketell of Dorsetshire. High Sheriff of Co. Monaghan in 1682. Killed at Drumbanagher on 13 March 1689
206	Ancketell	Richard	Ancketell Grove, Co. Monaghan	Brother of Mathew Ancketell (205)
207	Ancketell	Oliver	Ancketell Grove, Co. Monaghan	Son of Mathew Ancketell (205)
504	Anderson	Captain John	Co. Leitrim	
505	Anderson	John	Co. Cavan	
506	Anderson	James		
507	Anderson	Quartermaster W.		
1258	Andrews	Rev. John	Kinohir, Co. Fermanagh	
44	Annesley	Francis	Castlewellan, Co. Down	The first of the name in Ireland was Robert Annesley who acquired considerable estates in Counties Kerry and Down
1335	Anslow	Arthur	Co. Armagh	
491	Aplin	Captain Richard		
492	Aplin	Ensign Oliver		
198	Archdale	William	Castle Archdale, Co. Fermanagh	High Sheriff of County Fermanagh in 1667. Grandson of John Archdale of Norfolk who, in 1615, obtained a grant of land at Castle Archdale
576	Archer	Lieutenant Samuel		
233	Ardglass	Countess	Co. Down	Catherine, daughter of James Hamilton of Bangor married 4th Earl of Ardglass after death of her first husband, Richard Price (230).
641	Arkwright	Henry		
400	Armstrong	Captain		The Armstrongs were a well-known family in Co. Fermanagh

Young's ID	Surname	First Name	Residence	Remarks
401	Armstrong	Daniel	Co. Fermanagh	
402	Armstrong	Robert	Co. Fermanagh	
403	Armstrong	John		
404	Armstrong	Mathew		
405	Armstrong	Thomas		
406	Armstrong	Daniel		
407	Armstrong	Captain Martin		Distinguished himself at battle of Lisnaskea
8	Ash	Captain Thomas	Ashbrook, Glendermot, Co. Derry	His Siege Diary was published in 1792
9	Ash	Henry	Ashbrook, Glendermot, Co. Derry	Brother of Captain Thomas Ash. Mayor of Derry 1696, 1705 & 1709
10	Ash	Thomas	Ashfield, Co. Cavan	
1336	Assington	Rev. Thomas	Loughgall, Co. Armagh	
1001	Atkinson	Thomas	Ballyshannon, Co. Donegal	Grandson of Captain William Atkinson who settled in Ulster in Elizabeth's reign.
1002	Atkinson	Thomas junior	Ballyshannon, Co. Donegal	Son of Thomas Atkinson (1001). Died 1738.
1003	Atkinson	John	Co. Monaghan	Descended from an old Cumberland family which settled in Co. Monaghan at end of 16th century and which acquired considerable estate in Co. Fermanagh at Skea House, near Enniskillen.
986	Auchinleck	James	Ballaghinleck, Co. Fermanagh	Son of Rev. James Auchinleck (died 1680).
1474	Aunger	Rev. John	Co. Cavan	
1573	Austin	Jonathan	Derry	
1175	Ayerly	John	Manor Rod, Tyrone	
804	Babington	Mathew	Urney, Co. Tyrone	Grandson of Rev. Brutus Babington of Chester who was appointed Bishop of Derry in 1610 and died in 1611. Owner of estates of Urney, Co. Tyrone and Castle Doe, Co. Donegal
805	Babington	Captain William	Urney, Co. Tyrone and Castle Doe, Co. Don	Son of Mathew Babington (804). Led a small force to the assistance of Derry after the shutting of the gates.
806	Babington	Captain Richard	Limavady, Co. Derry and Lifford, Co. Doneg	
616	Bacon	Captain	Magilligan, Co. Derry	Son of Mathew Babington (804).
1206	Bagnall	Nicolas	Newry, Co. Down	Descended from an Elizabethan army officer who acquired considerable estate in Newry during the Tyrone wars (1594-1603). This family is represented by the Earl of Kilmorey.
1207	Bagnall	Thomas	Co. Cavan	
799	Bailey	Andrew		
800	Bailey	John		
801	Bailey	Robert	Tirnaskea, near Cookstown, Co. Tyrone	The family settled, at the Plantation, on the estate of Tirnaskea and erected a mansion house in 1632
802	Bailey	Alexander	Ringdufferin, Co. Down	Descendant of Alexander Bailie of Dochfour, Scotland who settled at Innishargie, Co. Down about 1600
803	Bailey	James	Innishargie, Co. Down	Descendant of Alexander Bailie of Dochfour, Scotland who settled at Innishargie about 1600
398	Baird	Robert		
2	Baker	Major Henry	Carrickfergus	Governor of Derry, nominated 19 April 1689. Died of fever 30 June 1689. Buried at St. Columb's Cathedral
450	Baker	Thomas		
1170	Baldington	Mathew	Donegal or Londonderry	
1577	Baldrick	William	Derry	
972	Balfour	Charles	Castle Balfour, Co. Fermanagh	Son of Sir William Balfour of Pitcullo, Scotland who purchased Castle Balfour estate in reign of Charles I which had been granted, at the Plantation, to Michael Balfour, Lord Balfour of Burleigh (in Kinross, Scotland) and his son Michael.
973	Balfour	William	Castle Balfour, Co. Fermanagh	Son of Charles Balfour (972)

Young's ID	Surname	First Name	Residence	Remarks
1260	Ball	William	Enniskillen, Co. Fermanagh	Son of Henry Ball, Provost of Enniskillen in 1668. Of an old Enniskillen family.
1261	Ball	John	Co. Armagh	
1475	Ballard	John	Co. Cavan	
1337	Barker	William	Co. Armagh	
1387	Barlow	Rev. Ralph	Co. Monaghan	
409	Barr	Tom		
410	Barr	Isabell		
446	Barrel	Captain	Urney, Strabane	
1388	Barret	Dacre	Co. Monaghan	
1523	Barrington	James	Derry	
837	Barry	John		
1259	Barton	William	Roe Island, Co. Fermanagh	Of an old Plantation family
427	Bashford	Captain Arthur	Co. Monaghan	
1208	Bates	Mathew	Down	
1246	Beaghan	Peter	Co. Antrim	
399	Beard	Robert	Armagh	
394	Beatty	Captain William	Moneymore, Co. Derry	Mentioned frequently in siege accounts for gallantry
395	Beatty	Mrs	Moneymore, Co. Derry	Mother of Captain William Beatty (394). Died in the city during the siege
1568	Beatty	Claud	Enniskillen	
963	Bedell	Ambrose	Co. Cavan	Grandson of Bishop Bedell who displayed much compassion during the 1641 rebellion and brother of Isabella Bedell, wife of Daniel French (961). Killed 19 April 1689
315	Bell	Captain Humphrey		
316	Bell	John	Co. Cavan	
317	Bell	Andrew	Co. Cavan	
324	Bennett	Joseph	Derry	Secretary to the Corporation of Derry
325	Bennett	Robert		
326	Bennett	Thomas		
1171	Benson	Basil	Donegal or Londonderry	Small landowners in neighbourhood of Culdaff, Co. Donegal
45	Beresford	Sir Tristram	Coleraine, Co. Derry	Grandson of Tristram, son of Michael Beresford of Orford, who was appointed agent for London City Companies in County Londonderry in early days of Plantation.
824	Berry	Lieutenant	Antrim	
1660	Berry	Lieutenant-Colonel William	England	Lieutenant-Colonel of the Enniskillen Horse at the Battle of the Boyne. Son of Major-General James Berry, of Devonshire, who served Cromwell during the English Civil War. The Berry family acquired Richhill Castle and estate in Co. Armagh.
1051	Betty	Adam	Carne, Co. Fermanagh	The family were long connected with the townland of Ballymillen, Ballinamallard, Co. Fermanagh
1052	Betty	John	Ardverney, Co. Fermanagh	
1053	Betty	Rowland	Ardverney, Co. Fermanagh	
547	Bickerstaffe	Captain John	Rosegift, Co. Antrim	
548	Bickerstaffe	Captain Richard	Rosegift, Co. Antrim	
1578	Bigland	James	Derry	
1054	Bingham	John senior	Co. Mayo	Probably son of Sir George Bingham of Foxford, Co. Mayo. The first of the family in Ireland was Elizabethan officer, Sir Richard Bingham of Sutton Bingham, Somersetshire.
1055	Bingham	Charles	Co. Mayo	
1056	Bingham	Charles	Co. Fermanagh	
1264	Bird (Brid)	Thomas	Lissaneskea, Co. Fermanagh	
1247	Black	John	Belfast, Co. Antrim	Of an old Plantation family, active with defenders of Enniskillen

Young's ID	Surname	First Name	Residence	Remarks
369	Black	Rev. Bartholomew	Aghaloo, Co. Tyrone	Rector of Aghaloo, Diocese of Armagh
259	Blacker	William	Carrick Blacker, Co. Armagh	Grandson of Valentine Blacker of Yorkshire who purchased the manor of Carrickblack in Loughgall in 1660 and son of George Blacker of Carrick Blacker, Sheriff of Co. Armagh in 1684.
1172	Blackwell	Quartermaster	Donegal or Londonderry	
989	Blackwood	John	Bangor, Co. Down	
990	Blackwood	John	Bangor, Co. Down	Son of John Blackwood (989). Married Ursula, daughter of Robert Hamilton of Killyleagh Castle and from whom descend the Viscounts of Clandeboye and Earls and Marquesses of Dufferin and Ava.
434	Blair	Colonel Thomas	Aghadowey (Agivey), Co. Derry	Served with distinction through siege. The Blair family were among the original settlers in the Agivey district.
435	Blair	Lieutenant David	Aghadowey (Agivey), Co. Derry	
436	Blair	James		Probably a son of Colonel Thomas Blair (434)
1530	Blair	Hugh	Enniskillen	
27	Blaney	Henry Vincent	Castle Blaney, Co. Monaghan.	The first of the name had received large grants in Monaghan at time of the Plantation.
1265	Boardman	John	Coolebey, Co. Fermanagh	Of an old Enniskillen family
612	Boid	Jean		
613	Boid	Isabel		
614	Boid	Robert		
615	Boid	Helen		
1576	Boner	Robert	Derry	
1575	Bonner	John	Derry	
1464	Booth	Robert	Co. Cavan	Yeoman
380	Boyd	Rev. Thomas	Aghadowey, Co. Derry	Presbyterian minister of Aghadowey
610	Boyd	Captain Francis		
611	Boyd	Captain James	Shipquay Street, Derry.	Killed by bomb falling on his house on 5 June 1689. The Boyd family, from Scotland, settled in the city of Derry and in Co. Donegal in the 17th century; they were in possession of the estate of Ballymacool near Letterkenny.
564	Boyer	Lieutenant Michael		
1248	Boyle	Alexander	Co. Antrim	
1341	Boyle	Robert	Co. Armagh	
1212	Boyse	John	Co. Down	
1029	Brabazon	Edward		4th Earl of Meath. Raised a regiment in support of King William. The first of the name in Ireland was Sir William Brabazon who was appointed Vice-Treasurer in 1534.
1030	Brabazon	James	Derry	An officer in Derry garrison in March 1689
569	Brady	Ensign John	Co. Monaghan	
570	Brady	John	Co. Monaghan	
571	Brady	Thomas	Co. Monaghan	
1209	Braton	John	Co. Tyrone	
1389	Brawshaw	John	Co. Monaghan	
605	Brazier	Colonel Kilner	Rath, Co. Donegal	Brought a large contingent of his tenantry for the defence of Derry. M.P. for St. Johnstown 1703-1713. First of the name, Paul Brazier settled in Coleraine at time of the Plantation and married a daughter of Sir Tristram Beresford.
357	Breme	Major		Killed by falling bombs on 5 June 1689
1070	Brett	William	Co. Down	The Brett family were originally settled in Lecale, where William Brett, High Sheriff of Co. Down in 1679, owned considerable property.
1071	Brett	Jasper	Co. Down	Son of William Brett (1070)
1072	Brett	Bernard	Co. Down	Son of William Brett (1070)

Young's ID	Surname	First Name	Residence	Remarks
1262	Briadon	Patrick	Derryboy, Co. Fermanagh	
1263	Briadon	William	Derry	
1391	Briaghan	Edward	Co. Monaghan	
1173	Brice	William	Letterkenny, Donegal	
1338	Bridges	Brook	Co. Armagh	
1339	Bright	John	Co. Armagh	
1340	Brightwell	Loftus	Co. Armagh	
792	Brisben	Rev. John		
1476	Brody	William	Co. Cavan	
239	Brooke	Captain Basil	Tullough Galloney, Co. Monaghan	Grandson of Basil Brooke, a distinguished Elizabethan officer who acquired, at the Plantation, large estate in Co. Donegal, and son of Henry Brooke, who for his services during the 1641 rebellion, received further large grants in Co. Fermanagh. Captain Basil Brooke succeeded to his father's Donegal property at Lough Eske.
240	Brooke	Thomas		Brother of Captain Basil Brooke (239). He succeeded to his father's Fermanagh property, married daughter of Sir John Cole and acquired the Cole estate which became known as Colebrooke.
241	Brooks	Henry	Co. Donegal or Londonderry	
242	Brooks	Lieutenant Edward	Co. Donegal or Londonderry	Sheriff of the city
358	Broom	Thomas		
331	Brown	Cornet		Killed in the Pennyburn Mill sortie of 21 April 1689
332	Brown	William		
386	Brown	Rev. David	Urney, Co. Tyrone	Presbyterian minister of Urney. Died in the city during the siege
1210	Brown	John	Co. Down	
1211	Brown	Alexander	Co. Down	
1390	Brown	William	Co. Monaghan	
359	Browne	Elizabeth		
335	Browning	Captain Micaiah	Derry	Captain of the Mountjoy and killed while breaking the boom across the Foyle
336	Browning	Captain William	Co. Fermanagh	
337	Browning	William	Enniskillen	
338	Browning	John		
339	Browning	James		
340	Browning	Mrs Margaret	Derry	Widow of Captain Micaiah Browning (335)
565	Brush	Ensign John		
622	Buchanan	John	Derry	As Deputy-Mayor of Derry in 1688 he opposed the shutting of the gates to prevent entry of Lord Antrim's Regiment.
623	Buchanan	James		
987	Buchanan	George	Enniskillen, Co. Fermanagh	First of the family in Ireland, settling at Omagh in 1674. Descended from the Buchanans of Carbeth, Scotland.
988	Buchanan	Marc	Enniskillen	
426	Bull	Major Nathaniel	Co. Meath	Distinguished himself in actions at Pennyburn Mill sortie of 21 April 1689 and Elagh sortie of 25 April 1689
1393	Bunden	James	Co. Monaghan	
1392	Burgess	Thomas	Co. Monaghan	
952	Burleigh	Captain Hercules	Carrickfergus, Co. Antrim	Son of William Burleigh of Carrickfergus. He served all through the siege of Derry. Died 1744
1176	Burley	John	Tyrone	
1518	Burnett	Thomas	Derry	
1177	Burney	John	Tyrone	

Young's ID	Surname	First Name	Residence	Remarks
639	Burnside	William	Derry	Appointed as a Protestant burgess by Tyrconnell to the new Corporation of Derry in 1688.
640	Burnside	John	Derry	
1544	Bury	Theo	Enniskillen	
1025	Butler	Francis	Co. Cavan	Son of Stephen Butler of Huntingdonshire, England who acquired, at the Plantation, a considerable estate near Newtownbutler, Co. Fermanagh. M.P. for Belturbet 1662 and 1692.
1026	Butler	Francis	Co. Fermanagh	Probably same person as 1025 with estates in both Cavan and Fermanagh
1027	Butler	Sir James	Co. Down	Probably son of Francis Butler (1025 & 1026)
158	Buttle	George	Glenarm, Co. Antrim	Son of Rev. David Buttle, Presbyterian minister of Ballymena, to which he came from Scotland in 1627
1174	Byers	George	Londonderry or Donegal	
1342	Byne	Henry	Co. Armagh	
1266	Byrney	William	Enniskillen, Co. Fermanagh	Of an old Enniskillen family
267	Cairnes	David	Knockmany, Killyfaddy manor, Co. Tyrone	Burgess and law agent to the Irish Society in Derry. Grandson of Alexander Cairnes, laird of Orchardston, Kirkcudbrighshire, Scotland who settled in Co. Donegal in 1609 and son of David who purchased in 1640 manor of Killyfaddy, Co. Tyrone. Prominent defender of the city during the siege. Died in 1722 and buried in St. Columb's Cathedral.
268	Cairnes	William	Killyfaddy, Co. Tyrone	Son of William Cairnes of Killyfaddy who was the brother of David Cairnes (267).
269	Cairnes	Colonel John	Claremore, Co.Tyrone	One of 13 apprentice boys who shut the gates on 8 December 1688
270	Cairnes	John	Agharononan, Co. Tyrone	
956	Caldwell	Sir James	Castle Rossbeg, Enniskillen, Co. Fermanagh	Son of John Caldwell of Stratton, near Prestwick, Scotland who came to Fermangah early in 17th century. Successful merchant in Enniskillen. Raised a regiment of foot and two troops of horse commanded by his sons, Hugh and John, which operated from Ballyshannon to Donegal town during the siege of Derry.
957	Caldwell	Elizabeth	Castle Rossbeg, Enniskillen, Co. Fermanagh	Daughter of Sir James Caldwell (956) who assisted in procuring supplies of powder and ball from Dublin merchant Mathew French (see 962) for the garrisons of Londonderry and Enniskillen.
958	Caldwell	Captain Hugh	Co. Fermanagh	Son of Sir James Caldwell (956).
959	Caldwell	Captain John	Co. Fermanagh	Son of Sir James Caldwell (956). Successfully defended Donegal Castle from attack by Duke of Berwick.
960	Caldwell	Charles	Co. Fermanagh	Son of Sir James Caldwell (956).
372	Campbell	Rev. John	Seagoe, Co. Armagh	Served in his father's foot regiment.
468	Campbell	Lieutenant-Colonel William		Rector of Seagoe, Diocese of Armagh
469	Campbell	Lieutenant Joshua		Sighted for bravery at Battle of Windmill Hill on 4 June 1689.
470	Campbell	John		
471	Campbell	Charles	Derry	
472	Campbell	David	Co. Down	
473	Campbell	Charles	Co. Down	
474	Campbell	William	Co. Down	
475	Campbell	Robert	Co. Down	
476	Campbell	David	Co. Cavan	
477	Campbell	Charles	Co. Leitrim	
478	Campbell	William	Co. Tyrone	
479	Campbell	James	Enniskillen	
480	Campbell	William	Enniskillen	

Young's ID	Surname	First Name	Residence	Remarks
632	Campsie	Alderman John	Derry	Mayor of Derry during the siege. John Campsie and his son Henry, as burgess, were among Protestant minority appointed by Tyrconnell to the new Corporation of Derry in 1688.
633	Campsie	John junior	Derry	Son of Alderman John Campsie (632)
635	Campsie	Major	Derry	The Campsies were an old mercantile family in Derry and surrounding district. Their name is preserved in a townland name in Faughanvale Parish on the river Faughan.
634	Campsie	Lieutenant Henry	Derry	Son of Alderman John Campsie (632). Appointed burgess by Tyrconnell in 1688 and one of 13 apprentices who shut the gates on 7 December 1688.
279	Canning	George	Garvagh, Co. Derry	Grandson of George Canning of Wiltshire who came to Ulster as agent to the Ironmongers' Company. Raised a regiment from the tenantry of his Garvagh estate which defended Coleraine and then Derry
1580	Carbwode	James	Derry	
729	Carey	Francis	Redcastle, Co. Donegal	Son of George Carey (died 1640) who was appointed Recorder of Derry in 1613 and acquired considerable estate at Redcastle, Inishowen.
730	Carey	Captain Francis	Redcastle, Co. Donegal	Son of Francis Carey (729)
731	Carey	Lieutenant William	Redcastle, Co. Donegal	Son of Francis Carey (729)
732	Carey	Colonel Edward	Dungiven, Co. Derry	Brother of Francis Carey (729)
733	Carey	Robert	Whitecastle	Probably son of Robert Carey of Whitecastle (died 1681) who was a brother of Francis Carey (729)
321	Carleton	Captain		
1557	Carleton	Christopher	Enniskillen	
1579	Carrigan	Charles	Derry	
1394	Carson	Charles	Co. Monaghan	
1178	Carton	Robert	Tyrone	
1267	Cashell	Lieutenant George	Co. Fermanagh	Fought with gallantry with the men of Enniskillen
1343	Castle	John	Co. Armagh	
757	Cathcart	Allen	Enniskillen, Co. Fermanagh	The Cathcarts were among the earliest settlers in the Enniskillen district
758	Cathcart	James	Enonisewry, Co. Fermanagh	
759	Cathcart	Hugh	Tullyshanlan, Co. Fermanagh	
760	Cathcart	Alex	Enonisewry, Co. Fermanagh	
761	Cathcart	Robert	Creaghmore, Co. Fermanagh	
762	Cathcart	Captain Malcolm	Enniskillen, Co. Fermanagh	Brother of Allen Cathcart (757)
763	Cathcart			
1268	Catlington	William	Enniskillen, Co. Fermanagh	
22	Caulfield	William	Castlecaulfield, Co. Tyrone	2nd Viscount Charlemont. At the Plantation, the first of the family in Ulster, Sir Tobias Caulfield, received large estates in Armagh and Tyrone
23	Caulfield	Captain Thomas	Castlecaulfield, Co. Tyrone	Seventh son of 2nd Viscount Charlemont.
1249	Chades	Henry	Belfast, Co. Antrim	
582	Chalmers	Captain James		
1344	Chaplain	Thomas	Co. Armagh	
318	Charleton	Captain		Deserted to the Jacobite camp on 28 July 1689.
319	Charleton	Charles	Co. Fermanagh	
320	Charlton	Randall	Co. Tyrone	
322	Charlton (or Carleton)	William	Co. Leitrim	
1269	Charters	Alexander	Co. Fermanagh	
1028	Chaworth	Viscount	Armagh	This refers to Patrick Chaworth, 2nd Viscount. The Chaworths originated from Annesley and Wiverton, Nottinghamsire, England
1345	Chemmick	Thomas	Co. Armagh	

Young's ID	Surname	First Name	Residence	Remarks
14	Chichester	Colonel John	Dungannon, Co. Tyrone	Second son of Colonel John Chichester of Dungannon, brother of Arthur Chichester the first Earl of Donegall. The Chichesters were from Devonshire.
1346	Chiney	Thomas	Co. Armagh	
1270	Chittie (Chittoge)	Thomas	Enniskillen, Co. Fermanagh	
1179	Christall	John	Tyrone	
374	Christy	Rev. James	Monaghan	Curate of Monaghan, Diocese of Clogher
235	Church	Captain William	Coleraine	The Church family settled at Oatlands, near Coleraine in the early 17th century. Killed in sortie of 27 May 1689. Buried in St. Columb's Cathedral
236	Church	William	Coleraine	
237	Church	George	Coleraine	Brother of William Church (235)
144	Clark	Mathew	Largantogher, Maghera, Co. Derry	Only connected to the Siege by marriage. The first of the family to settle in Ulster was John Clark from Lancashire who took a lease of land from Drapers' Compnay in 1690
145	Clarke	Edward	Derry	
146	Clarke	John	Co.Monaghan	
147	Clarke	Samuel	Armagh	
148	Clarke	Alderman	Armagh	
149	Clarke	George	Armagh	
150	Clarke	George	Armagh	
151	Clarke	Robert	Armagh	
152	Clarke		Co. Fermanagh	
361	Clarke	Lieutenant Mathew		Ordained Presbyterian minister of Boveedy in 1697 and succeeded Rev. James McGregor (360) as minister of Londonderry, New Hampshire in 1729.
1347	Cleegston	Thomas	Co. Armagh	
649	Cleland	Abigail		
588	Clements	Henry	Straid, Carrickfergus	Clements family settled in Carrickfergus from 1609.
589	Clements	Edward	Straid, Carrickfergus	Brother of Henry Clements (588). Mayor of Carrickfergus in 1696. The Clements brothers together with 21 other gentry of Co. Antrim raised regiments in defence of Protestant interests.
590	Clements	Ensign John		
591	Clements	Dalway		
592	Clements	Robert	Co. Cavan	
1250	Cleyston	Robert	Belfast, Co. Antrim	
1136	Clifford	Edward	Co. Donegal	
539	Closs	Two Captains		
1348	Clutterbuck	Richard	Co. Armagh	
1137	Coach	Thomas	Co.Donegal	
1477	Coach	Thomas	Co. Cavan	
421	Cochran	Elizabeth		
420	Cochran	Jean		
417	Cochrane	Robert		
419	Cochrane	Thomas		
669	Cockayne	Alderman Mathew		Ceased to be an alderman when Tyrconnell revoked the old charter in 1688. The Cockaynes were one of the great mercantile families of the City of London at beginning of 17th century and Sir William Cockayne was the first Governor of the Irish Society.
670	Cockayne	Charles		4th Viscount Cullen who was summoned to James' Dublin Parliament in 1689. Great great-grandson of London merchant, Sir William Cockayne who in 1613 became first Governor of the Irish Society
422	Coghan	Peller		

Young's ID	Surname	First Name	Residence	Remarks
416	Coghran	Captain John	Belrath, Armagh	It was in Captain Coghran's old residence that a copy of Aicken's extensive poem about the siege (i.e. Londeriados) was discovered in 1790 (11).
418	Coghran	Marmaduke		
568	Colburn	James		
918	Cole	Thomas	Co. Monaghan	Probably a member of the Cole family of Florence Court
919	Cole	Lieutenant Francis	Ballyleck, Co. Monaghan	
920	Cole	Colonel Richard	Ballyleck, Co. Monaghan	
921	Cole	William	Colehill, Co. Fermanagh	
922	Cole	Sir Arthur	Co. Tyrone	Grandson of Captain William Cole (died 1653) who, at the Plantation, received large grants of land in neighbourhood of Enniskillen Castle, settled at Florence Court, built the town of Enniskillen and defended Enniskillen in 1641 rebellion.
1548	Collyer	Isaac	Enniskillen	
451	Colquhoun	Charles	Letterkenny	
452	Colquhoun	James	Co. Fermanagh	Sir John Colquhoun, Laird of Luss, Scotland was one of the original grantees of 1000 acres in Co. Donegal
1180	Colson	Thomas	Tyrone	
112	Colville	Sir Robert	Newtown, Co. Down and Galgorm Castle.	Grandson of Alexander Colville of Culross, Scotland. Sir Robert's father came to Ulster c. 1615 and purchased the Galgorm estate in 1627.
453	Comyn		Lifford, Co. Donegal	Aged over 80. Claimed the right as the oldest man on the walls to fire the first shot at King James as he sought the city's surrender on 18 April 1689
1525	Conlay	Thomas	Derry	
1089	Conolly	Patrick	Ballyshannon, Co. Donegal	Patrick's son was William Conolly of Castletown, Speaker of the Irish House of Commons, who acquired a huge fortune, with estates in 13 Irish counties. William Conolly bought, in 1691, the manor of Limavady, Co. Derry from George Phillips. Connected to Sir Foulke Conway, an Elizabethan officer, who was granted a large estate on the south-east of Lough Neagh which included the town of Lisburn. In 1683 the Killultagh estate was left to a cousin, Popham Seymour on condition of assuming the name of Conway.
953	Conway (Seymour)	Popham	Killultagh estate, Co. Antrim	
159	Conyngham	Colonel William	Ballydrum, now Springhill, Moneymore, Co. Derry	Grandson of William Cunningham who came from Scotland and settled at Ballydrum in 1609
160	Conyngham	Colonel William	Ballydrum, now Springhill, Moneymore, Co. Derry	
161	Conyngham	Colonel William	Ballydrum, now Springhill, Moneymore, Co. Derry	
162	Conyngham	Sir Albert	Mount Charles, Co. Donegal	Grandson of Rev. Alexander Conyngham who settled in Donegal in 1611.
163	Conyngham	Henry	Mount Charles, Co. Donegal	Son of Sir Albert Conyngham (162)
218	Cook	Lieutenant	Lisnagarvey, Lisburn, Co. Down	
896	Cooke	Rev.	Co. Donegal	
897	Cooke	George	Derry	
1271	Cooper	Captain	Co. Monaghan	
1272	Cooper	George		Probably the same person as 1271. Captain in the local Enniskillen forces
1273	Cooper	Alexander	Co. Monaghan	
1274	Cooper	James	Co. Monaghan	A family with considerable standing in Enniskillen and surrounding counties. A William Cooper was Provost of Enniskillen in 1674 and 1677.
1133	Coote	Captain Chidley	Co. Carlow	Commander of Protestant troops raised in Sligo in Spring 1689. Assisted men of Enniskillen in their preparations for defence.
1134	Coote	Captain Thomas	Co. Monaghan	
1135	Coote	Thomas	Co. Cavan	
1009	Cope	Downham	Drumilly, Co. Armagh	The first of the family in Ireland was Sir Anthony Cope of Hanwell, Berkshire who, at the Plantation, were granted estates in Co. Armagh at Drumilly and Loughgall.

Young's ID	Surname	First Name	Residence	Remarks
1010	Cope	Henry	Loughgall, Co. Armagh	
1465	Coplin	William	Co. Cavan	Yeoman
1466	Coplin	William junior	Co. Cavan	Son of William Coplin (1465)
1508	Cormac	Richard	Derry	
1395	Corners	John senior	Co. Monaghan	
1396	Corners	John junior	Co. Monaghan	
1181	Cornwall	John	Tyrone	
289	Corry	Captain James	Castle Coole, Enniskillen, Co. Fermanagh	Son of John Corry who purchased Castlecoole estate in 1656
290	Corry	Nathaniel	Glaan, Co. Monaghan	
291	Corry	Isaiah	Glaan, Co. Monaghan	
292	Corry	Samuel	Glaan, Co. Monaghan	
293	Corry	Walter	Co. Monaghan	
294	Corry	William	Co. Donegal or Londonderry	
295	Corry	John	Castle Coole, Enniskillen, Co. Fermanagh	Son of Captain James Corry (289)
296	Corry	Hugh	Enniskillen	
297	Corry	George	Enniskillen	
298	Corry	Captain James	Ballyclanara, Co. Monaghan	
1275	Cosby	Captain Arnold	Co. Cavan	He was a member of the family of Lismore, Co. Cavan. As an 'officer of local horse' he was prominent among the men of Enniskillen.
1276	Cosby	Edward		
1213	Cosslett	Charles	Co. Down	
1467	Cotnam	Abraham	Co. Cavan	Yeoman
219	Cowan	Captain John	St. Johnstown, Derry	
220	Cowan	Robert		
1397	Cozens	John	Co. Monaghan	
1252	Cragg	William	Glenarm, Co. Antrim	
630	Craig	Alderman	Derry	Ceased to be an alderman when Tyrconnell revoked the old charter in 1688.
631	Craige	William		
1581	Crane	Thomas	Derry	
1138	Crawford	John	Donegal, Londonderry	
1139	Crawford	William	Donegal, Londonderry	
1251	Crawford	Quartermaster Thomas	Belfast, Co. Antrim	
1277	Crawford	Laurence	Cravencarry, Co. Fermanagh	
946	Creighton	Abraham	Crom Castle, Co. Fermanagh	Son of Abraham Creighton (died 1631) of Frindraught, Aberdeenshire, Scotland who settled, at the Plantation, at Dromdoory, Co. Fermanagh. Acquired the Crom Castle estate and defended Crom Castle successfully on 2 occasions from Jacobite forces during 1689. Sheriff in 1673. M.P. in 1692. Died in 1705
947	Creighton	James	Crom Castle, Co. Fermanagh	Son of Abraham Creighton (946). A distinguished captain in his father's regiment. Died 1701.
948	Creighton	John	Crom Castle, Co. Fermanagh	Son of James Creighton (947).
949	Creighton	David	Crom Castle, Co. Fermanagh	Brother of James Creighton (947). Distinguished himself in successful defence of Crom Castle from Jacobite forces in 1689, and in the Williamite Wars as an officer in King William's army.
950	Creighton	Alexander	Lissancara, Co. Fermanagh	
1468	Crigg	Robert	Co. Cavan	Yeoman
430	Crofton	Colonel Richard	Lisdorn, Co. Roscommon	
431	Crofton	Franck	Lisdorn, Co. Roscommon	Brother of Colonel Richard Crofton (430)
432	Crofton	John	Lisdorn, Co. Roscommon	Brother of Colonel Richard Crofton (430)
1349	Crofton	Edward	Co. Armagh	

Young's ID	Surname	First Name	Residence	Remarks
579	Crofts	Adjutant William		Messenger of the relieving force who swam up the river. Reached the garrison
709	Cromie	James	Ballymoney, Co. Antrim	
711	Crommy	John	Co. Monaghan	
1398	Cron	Ensign Christopher	Ballykelly, Co. Derry	
381	Crooks	Rev. William		Presbyterian minister of Ballykelly
486	Crooks	Captain John		Secured victory at Battle of Windmill Hill on 4 June 1689
487	Crooks	Captain William		Died of wounds at end of April 1689
713	Crookshanks	Lieutenant William	Derry	One of 13 apprentice boys who shut the gates on 7 December 1688. Elected Burgess of Corporation in October 1689. Appointed Sheriff in 1692
714	Crookshanks	John	Derry	One of 4 Protestant Burgesses appointed by Tyrconnell to the new Corporation of Derry in 1688.
1519	Crosland	George	Derry	
627	Cross	John	Co. Tyrone	
628	Cross	William	Co. Tyrone	
1562	Crowe	Laurence	Enniskillen	
377	Crowther	Rev. Richard	Cumber, Co. Derry	Curate of Cumber, Diocese of Derry. Died in the city during the siege
1007	Crozier	John	Co. Fermanagh	The Croziers had been settled for many generations at Gortra, Co. Fermanagh, and at Rockview, Co. Cavan.
1008	Crozier	John	Co. Fermanagh	
710	Crumy	John		
1478	Culme	Arthur	Co. Cavan	
1583	Cuming	Thomas	Derry	
164	Cunningham	John	Tully, Co. Donegal	
165	Cunningham	Alexander	Derry	One of 13 apprentice boys who shut the gates on 7 December 1688.
166	Cunningham	Lieutenant Joseph	Kilmacenet, Co. Antrim	
167	Cunningham	Lieutenant John		
168	Cunningham	Captain Michael	Prehen, Co. Derry	Prehen was later sold to the Knoxes
169	Cunningham	Captain John		Killed at Windmill Hill on 6 May 1689
170	Cunningham	James Roe		
171	Cunningham	James	Derry	
172	Cunningham	Archibald	Derry	
174	Cunningham	Colonel John		Commander of English Regiment that arrived in the Foyle on 15 April 1689 but returned to England on 18th April without landing stores and munitions. Court-martialed
495	Curling	Quartermaster Edward	Derry	Storekeeper of provisions
835	Curry	James	Derry	
836	Curry	Edward	Derry	
818	Cust	Henry	Magilligan, Co. Derry	
1582	Cuthbert	Henry	Derry	
1659	Cutts	General	England	With a great reputation for bravery and as commander of an English regiment in the Dutch service he served King William in his campaigns in Ireland and Flanders.
1588	Daglish	John	Derry	
516	Dalton	Lieutenant		
514	Dalzell	Lieutenant		Artillery Officer on church steeple
1049	Dane	Paul	Enniskillen	Son of John Dane of Devonshire who settled in Fermanagh in 1647. Provost of Enniskillen, 1688-89
1050	Dane	John	Enniskillen	Son of Paul Dane (1049). Officer in the Enniskillen Horse and Provost of Enniskillen in 1690
1350	Daniel	Not recorded	Co. Armagh	

Young's ID	Surname	First Name	Residence	Remarks
1453	D'Arcy	Abraham	Co. Monaghan	
1454	D'Arcy	Patrick	Co. Monaghan	
1182	Darragh	Andrew	Tyrone	
1351	Daunt	Achilles	Co. Armagh	
1531	Davenport	Edward	Co. Donegal	The Davenports were a Co. Donegal Plantation family. Probably refugees in Enniskillen.
1532	Davenport	Thomas	Co. Donegal	The Davenports were a Co. Donegal Plantation family. Probably refugees in Enniskillen.
888	Daveys	Hugh	Derry	
1585	Davidson	William	Derry	
367	Davis	Rev. Moses	Donagheny, Co. Tyrone	Rector of Donagheny, Diocese of Armagh
889	Davis	Nathaniel	Derry	
890	Davis	Jean	Derry	
891	Davis	Jane	Co. Fermanagh	
892	Davis	Captain Edward	Co. Fermanagh	
893	Davis	James	Carrickfergus, Co. Antrim	
894	Davis	Hercules	Co. Antrim	The Davys family were long connected with Carrickfergus. A Cromwellian officer of the name later settled near Cullybackey.
895	Davis	Captain Hercules	Co. Antrim	Son of Hercules Davis (894).
1586	Davison	Walter	Derry	
887	Davys	Edward		
130	Dawson		Moyola Park, Castledawson, Co. Derry	The Dawsons were planters from Westmorland, England. In 1633, Thomas Dawson purchased Castledawson estate from Sir Thomas Phillips. The Dawsons had no direct connection with the Siege, only through marriage to Chichester Clarks.
131	Dawson	John		
132	Dawson	Walter		
134	Dawson	John	Killcroe, Co. Monaghan	Burgess of Armagh, died 1691
135	Dawson	Captain Walter	Dawson's Grove	Grandson of John Dawson (134)
136	Dawson	Captain Richard	Dawson's Grove	A retired Cromwellian officer
137	Dawson	Isaac	Dromany, Co. Monaghan	
138	Dawson	Lancelot	Killcroe, Co. Monaghan	
139	Dawson	William	Killcroe, Co. Monaghan	
133	Dawson	Walter Junior		
513	Delap	James	Enniskillen	
509	Delapp	James senior	Enniskillen, Co. Fermanagh	
510	Delapp	James junior	Enniskillen, Co. Fermanagh	
511	Delapp	Frances	Moylagh, Co. Donegal	
512	Delapp	Robert	Ballyshannon, Co. Donegal	
1509	Denniston	Robert	Derry	
1140	Denny	William	Londonderry	
1587	Derring	Neeve	Derry	
1555	Devitt	James	Enniskillen	
1004	Dixie	Rev. Edward	Co. Cavan	Dean of Kilmore, Co. Cavan
1005	Dixie	Lieutenant Edward	Co. Monaghan	Son of Rev. Edward Dixie (1004). Defender of Enniskillen
1006	Dixie	Captain Woolstan		Son of Rev. Edward Dixie (1004). An officer of the Enniskillen Horse who was captured defending his father's deanery near Belturbet. Executed by orders of Lord Galmoy (Piers Butler) who raised and led a regiment of horse in the Jacobite army.
795	Dixon	Captain John		Sheriff of Derry in 1697

Young's ID	Surname	First Name	Residence	Remarks
1352	Dixon	Robert	Co. Armagh	Probably Captain Dixon (795)
606	Dobbin	Major John	Carrowdonaghey, Ahoghill, Co. Antrim	
607	Dobbin	Captain C.		
608	Dobbin	William		
609	Dobbin	Anthony		The Dobbin family were long settled at Carrickfergus. Peter Dobbin was Constable of Carrickfergus Castle in 1400. The Dobbins acquired considerable property in Co. Antrim at Ahoghill, Duneane and Drumseugh
216	Dobbs	John	Co. Monaghan	The first of the name in Ulster was John Dobbs who came over from Yorkshire in 1580 as an officer in the Carrickfergus garrison. The family acquired considerable property in Carrickfergus from end of 16th century.
217	Dobbs	Captain Richard	Castle Dobbs, Carrickfergus, Co. Antrim	The Donaldsons were a branch of the Macdonnells of the Glens. High Sheriff of County Antrim in 1665. One of 23 gentry of Co. Antrim who raised regiments in defence of Protestant interests in the county.
945	Donaldson	John	Glenarm, Co. Antrim	
15	Donegall	2nd Earl	Dungannon, Co. Tyrone	The 2nd Earl was Arthur Chichester, the eldest son of John Chichester of Dungannon
16	Donegall	Countess Letitia	Dungannon, Co. Tyrone	Dowager of 1st Earl of Donegall
1543	Donellan	Cor	Enniskillen	
346	Douglas	Captain Andrew	Coleraine	Captain of the Phoenix of Coleraine which relieved Derry
347	Douglas	Lieutenant		Killed at Windmill Hill on 6 May 1689
1653	Douglas	General James	Scotland	Commanded the Scots Guards at the Boyne. Killed at Steinkirk, in William's Flanders campaign, in 1692
515	Downing	Lieutenant-Colonel Adar	Rosegift, Bellaghy, Co. Derry	
642	Draper	William		
1455	Drope	Bartholomew	Carrowaskey, Co. Monaghan	
1569	Drury	George	Enniskillen	Lieutenant in local force
1570	Drury	Robert	Callow, Co. Roscommon	Probably a refugee in Enniskillen from Callow, Co. Roscommon
1584	Dun	William	Derry	
191	Dunbar		Derrygonnelly, Co. Fermanagh	Among the first settlers at the Plantation was John Dunbar of Mochram, Wigtownshire, Scotland. The Dunbars acquired by purchase the large estate of Derrygonnelly near Enniskillen. By marriage the Derrygonnelly estate passed into the Montgomery family.
192	Dunbar	Thomas	Enniskillen, Co. Fermanagh	
193	Dunbar	John	Killoe, Co. Fermanagh	
194	Dunbar	John	Ballinure, Co. Fermanagh	
195	Dunbar	Philip	Derry	
196	Dunbar	Captain		
197	Dunbar	Lieutenant Andrew		
1278	Dundas	James	Enniskillen, Co. Fermanagh	A member of a landed family prominent in Enniskillen and surrounding counties
508	Dunlop	Lieutenant		A branch of this Ayrshire family, variously spelt as Dunlop and Delap, settled on Lough Swilly, Co. Donegal in the early years of the plantation
680	Eadie	Hugh		
1141	Earls	Francis	Ballyshannon, Londonderry	
1253	Eaton	Captain William	Dunfane, Co. Antrim	
1279	Eccles	Charles	Fintona, Co. Tyrone	
1280	Eccles	Captain Samuel	Co. Monaghan	
1281	Eccles	Samuel	Co. Tyrone	
1282	Eccles	Daniel		Son of Gilbert Eccles who settled in Fermanagh in Charles I's reign and acquired manors of Shannon and Rathmoran, near Clones, and of Castlelee, near Fintona.

Young's ID	Surname	First Name	Residence	Remarks
1469	Echenby	Peter	Co. Cavan	Yeoman
105	Echlin	Robert	Ardquin, Co. Down	
106	Echlin	John	Ardquin, Co. Down	Son of Robert Echlin (105)
107	Echlin	Captain Robert	Ardquin, Co. Down	Son of Robert Echlin (105)
108	Echlin	Dean Robert		Dean of Tuam
1479	Edgeworth	Henry	Co. Cavan	
109	Edmonstone	Archibald	Redhall, Co. Antrim	The grandson of Archibald Edmonstone, Laird of Duntreath, Stirlingshire, who bought a considerable estate in County Antrim in 1617, near Carrickfergus.
1142	Edwards	Captain Nicholas	Kilrea, Co. Derry	
681	Edy	Thomas	Co. Tyrone	
682	Edy	Thomas	Co. Tyrone	
376	Ellingsworth	Rev.	Newry, Co. Down	Died in the city during the siege
1285	Elliott	Thomas	Galoone, Co. Fermanagh	Probably the same person as 1284.
1286	Elliott	Robert	Storchin, Co. Fermanagh	
1287	Elliott	James	Storchin, Co. Fermanagh	
1288	Elliott	William	Storaghin, Co. Leitrim	
1289	Ellis	Thomas	Co. Monaghan	
1290	Ellis	Edward	Enniskillen, Co. Fermanagh	
1291	Ellis	Augustus	Enniskillen, Co. Fermanagh	
1292	Ellis	Francis	Enniskillen, Co. Fermanagh	
1293	Ellis	Hercules	Enniskillen, Co. Fermanagh	
769	Ellison	George		
1283	Ellit	George	Tully, Co. Fermanagh	
1284	Ellit	Thomas	Galoone, Co. Fermanagh	
906	Erwin			By tradition, son of Cornet Erwin who distinguished himself in 1641 rebellion. Cornet Erwin refers to Sir Gerard Irvine (Erwin) who was son of Christopher Irvine (who died 1666), the original grantee of Castle Irvine estate, Co. Fermanagh. The Irvines were descended from Irvine of Bonshaw, Dumfries, Scotland.
1183	Evans	Captain Adam	Tyrone	
1353	Evelyn	John	Co. Armagh	
1524	Everett	Henry	Derry	
1294	Evett	Richard	Magherastephenagh, Co. Fermanagh	
704	Evins	Lieutenant		
705	Evory	George	Londonderry	
1589	Evory	William	Derry	
1537	Ewart	James	Enniskillen	Provost of Enniskillen in 1684
683	Ewing	Sam		
684	Ewing	Joshua		
685	Ewing	John		
686	Ewing	Jean		
1214	Facely	Hugh	Co. Down	
1511	Fane	Richard	Derry	
1295	Farquhar	Alexander	Co. Fermanagh	
1143	Farrard	William	Donegal, Londonderry	
1215	Farrer	Captain John	Co. Down	
208	Ferguson	Lieutenant Samuel	Derry	The first Ferguson was Rev. Andrew Ferguson, Presbyterian minister of Burt, Co. Donegal in middle of 17th century.
1399	Ferguson	David	Co. Monaghan	
1400	Fish	Richard	Co. Monaghan	

Young's ID	Surname	First Name	Residence	Remarks
154	Fisher	James	Donegal or Londonderry	
156	Fisher	Lieutenant	Monaghan	
157	Fisher	John	Donegal or Londonderry	Brother of James Fisher (154)
155	Fisher	Daniel	Co. Monaghan	
1401	Fitzsimons	Rev. Thomas		
1031	Fitzwilliam	William		2nd Baron of Lifford. Descended from Sir William Fitzwilliam of Milton, Yorkshire who was appointed Lord Deputy of Ireland in 1584.
560	Fleming	James		
561	Fleming	Richard	Ballymagorry, Co. Tyrone	
562	Fleming	John		
1403	Flinton	Fulke	Co. Monaghan	
28	Folliott	Lord	Ballyshannon, Co. Donegal	3rd Baron of Ballyshannon. His grandfather Sir Henry Folliott purchased the large Ballyshannon estate in the early Plantation years
29	Folliott	Captain John	Ballyshannon, Co. Donegal	
30	Folliott	Thomas	Ballyshannon, Co. Donegal	
31	Folliott	Francis	Ballyshannon, Co. Donegal	
559	Forbes			
1144	Forker	Rev. John	Co. Donegal	
1296	Forster	John	Carnemackasker, Co. Fermanagh	
1297	Forster	Rev. John	Co. Monaghan	
1298	Forster	Captain Francis	Co. Monaghan	
1299	Forster	Andrew	Drumgorme, Co. Fermanagh	
951	Fortescue	Colonel Chichester	Donoughmore, Co. Down	Grandson of Sir Faithful Fortescue of Buckland Filleigh, Devonshire who came to Ireland in 1604 and acquired considerable estates at Dromisken, Co. Louth; Donoughmore, Co. Down; and Galgorm Castle, Co. Antrim. Raised a troop of horse for defence of Derry.
1547	Forth	Samuel	Enniskillen	Captain in Wolseley's Horse. Wounded at the Boyne and Aughrim
203	Forward	John	Burt, Co. Donegal	
204	Forward	Captain John	Burt, Co. Donegal	Son of John Forward (203) and grandson of Rev. William Forward who first acquired land in Burt, Castle Forward, in 1640.
1402	Fox	Sergeant William	Co. Monaghan	
17	Franklin	Sir William	Belfast, Co. Antrim	Of Moverne, Bedfordshire. Represented the interests of the Donegall family in Co. Antrim
1354	Frazer	Alexander	Co. Armagh	
1590	Freear	Helenor	Derry	
558	Freeman	Captain		
961	French	Daniel	Belturbet, Co. Cavan	Son of Mathew French. Assisted with the defence of Enniskillen
962	French	Mathew	Belturbet, Co. Cavan	Brother of Daniel French (961). A Dublin merchant who supplied arms and ammunition to his brother Daniel in Belturbet for use by garrisons of Londonderry and Enniskillen. High Sheriff of Co. Fermanagh in 1677.
1571	Frith	William	Enniskillen	
1301	Frizell	Jo.	Enniskillen, Co. Fermanagh	
1300	Frizzel	George	Co. Monaghan	
1521	Fuller	John	Derry	
620	Fullerton	Ralph		
621	Fullerton	John	Ballegh, Co. Antrim	Probably related to George Fullerton of Ballintoy Castle
1535	Fulton	James	Enniskillen	Captain in local forces
1536	Fulton	Andrew	Enniskillen	Lieutenant in local forces
1355	Gaffikin	John	Co. Armagh	
1145	Gage	John	Magilligan, Londonderry	

Young's ID	Surname	First Name	Residence	Remarks
863	Galbraith	Robert	Clonabogan, Omagh, Co. Tyrone	The family, from Scotland, settled early in the 17th century in Co. Tyrone where they soon acquired considerable estate
864	Galbraith	Elizabeth	Clonabogan, Omagh, Co. Tyrone	
865	Galbraith	John	Co. Leitrim	
866	Galbraith	Robert	Co. Leitrim	
867	Galbraith	Robert	Co. Fermanagh	
868	Galbraith	Hugh	Enniskillen	
869	Galbraith	John	Enniskillen	
466	Gallagher	Captain James	Bishop Street, Derry	
840	Galland	Captain Michael	Vow, Co. Antrim	Son of Captain John Galland, an officer in Cromwell's army who obtained a grant of land at the Vow, near Ballymoney, at time of Cromwellian settlement.
841	Galland	Benjamin	Vow, Co. Antrim	Brother of Captain Michael Galland (840)
756	Galtworth	James		
1596	Gamble	William	Derry	
1085	Gardiner	William K.	Derry	William Gardner was Mayor of Derry in 1662.
1082	Gardner	Henry	Co. Antrim	The Gardners were a prominent family in Derry and neighbouring counties.
1083	Gardner	Henry	Co. Down	
1084	Gardner	Alex	Derry	
706	Garnett	George		
1184	Garvan	William	Tyrone	
1594	Getty	James	Derry	
1404	Gibb	George	Co. Monaghan	
1356	Gibbs	William	Co. Armagh	
1216	Gibson	Rev. Michael	Co. Down	
1254	Gibson	Robert	Co. Down	
1480	Gibson	Richard	Co. Cavan	
1481	Gibson	Bar.	Enniskillen, Co. Fermanagh	
1595	Gifford	Christopher	Derry	
385	Gilchrist	Rev. William	Kilrea, Co. Derry	Presbyterian minister of Kilrea. Died in the city during the siege
1146	Gillespie	James	Londonderry	
1591	Gilling	John	Derry	
1357	Gills	John	Co. Armagh	
1405	Gilmore	John	Co. Monaghan	
1656	Ginkell	General	Holland	Served with distinction, in William's Irish campaign, at the Boyne, Athlone, Aughrim and Limerick. In recognition of his services he was created Earl of Athlone.
1147	Glasgow	Thomas	Donegal	
544	Gledstanes	Captain James	Fardross, Clogher, Co. Tyrone	The Gledstanes family in possession of Fardross since early 17th century.
545	Gledstanes	Captain John	Fardross, Clogher, Co. Tyrone	Brother of Captain James Gledstanes (544)
567	Goburn	Lieutenant		
481	Godfrey	Captain Stephen	Coleraine	
482	Godfrey	Warren		
483	Godfrey	William	Castleroe, Co. Donegal	
484	Godfrey	Thomas	Derry	
485	Godfrey	John	Derry	
1561	Golden	James	Screen, Co. Sligo	Probably a refugee in Enniskillen from Screen, Co. Sligo
1185	Goodlet	William	Tyrone	
13	Gordon	Rev. James	Glendermot, Co. Derry	Presbyterian minister of Glendermot
496	Gordon	Joseph		
497	Gordon	Colonel Joseph	Co. Tyrone	

Young's ID	Surname	First Name	Residence	Remarks
498	Gordon	Alexander	Derry	
1011	Gore	Sir William	Manor Gore, Co. Donegal	Married daughter and heiress of Sir James Hamilton of Manor Hamilton, Co. Tyrone.
1012	Gore	Ralph	Manor Gore, and Manor Hamilton, Co. Tyro	Son of Sir William Gore (1011).
1013	Gore	Sir Francis		Served gallantly with the men of Enniskillen in defending the town. Booth Gores of Lissadell, Co. Sligo are descended from Sir Francis Gore.
550	Gorges	Henry	Somerset, Londonderry	Probably a son of Colonel John Gorges, Mayor of Derry in 1661
537	Gow	Thomas		
776	Graham	Alderman James	Derry	
777	Graham	James	Ballashule, Donegal or Londonderry	
778	Graham	James junior	Ballashule, Donegal or Londonderry	
779	Graham	Captain		
780	Graham	Major		Died as result of beng struck by cannon ball at Shipquay Gate on 5 June.
781	Graham	John	Derry	The family were of the clan expelled from the Scottish Borders in the 17th century.
782	Graham		Co. Leitrim	A John Graham was Sheriff of Derry in 1662
783	Graham	Lieutenant John	Glasslough, Co. Monaghan	
784	Graham	Francis	Enniskillen	
785	Graham	James	Enniskillen	
1186	Grayson	John	Tyrone	
1187	Grayson	Henry	Tyrone	
499	Green	Lieutenant		
500	Green	Ralph	Derry	
501	Green	Christopher	Derry	
502	Greene	Rev. William	Killeter, Co. Fermanagh	
540	Gregory	Captain Robert	Coleraine	
541	Gregory	Lieutenant	Coleraine	Son of Captain Robert Gregory (540)
542	Gregory	Ensign	Coleraine	Son of Captain Robert Gregory (540)
543	Gregory	Captain George	Coleraine	Brother of Captain Robert Gregory (540)
1510	Gregson	Andrew	Derry	
1592	Grier	John	Derry	
970	Griffith	Lieutenant Henry		
1217	Griffith	John	Co. Down	
1593	Grigg	William	Derry	
238	Grove	Captain William	Castle Shannaghan, Co. Donegal	On the shutting of the gates Captain Grove answered Derry's appeal by bringing in a troop of his own tenants from Kilmacrenan
1482	Groylins	Henry	Co. Cavan	
1539	Gubin	Edward	Enniskillen	
654	Guest	John	Belfast, Co. Antrim	
1406	Gun	John	Co. Monaghan	
1407	Gun	William	Co. Cavan	
549	Gunter	Lieutenant William		
1515	Guthridge	Thomas	Derry	
1483	Gwylim	Captain Meredith	Co. Cavan	
734	Gwynn	William	Derry	
735	Gwynn	James	Derry	
736	Gwynn	Mary	Derry	
585	Gyford	Ensign George		
1081	Hackett	Rt. Rev. Thomas	Hammersmith	Bishop of Down and Connor
1218	Haddock	John	Co. Down	

Young's ID	Surname	First Name	Residence	Remarks
766	Haire	James		
1219	Halbridge	William	Co. Down	
629	Hall	Albert		Died 1701 and buried in Cathedral graveyard
1302	Hall	John	Enniskillen, Co. Fermanagh	
1220	Hall	Roger	Co. Down	Ancestor of the Halls of Narrow Water, Co. Down
1188	Hallow	John	Tyrone	
1516	Halston	John	Derry	
428	Hamill	Colonel Hugh	Lifford, Co. Donegal	Hamill raised a regiment among his tenantry and neighbours to defend Derry during the siege. Died in 1721. Buried in Old Glendermot graveyard.
429	Hamill	William	Lifford, Co. Donegal	Brother of Colonel Hugh Hamill (428)
383	Hamill	Rev. John	Donagheady, Co. Tyrone	Presbyterian minister of Donagheady. Died in the city during the siege
1090	Hamilton	Captain James	Co. Tyrone	Served with distinction through the Siege. Grandson of Sir George Hamilton of Dunnalong and Great-grandson of the 1st Earl of Abercorn who became 6th Earl of Abercorn in 1701. The Hamiltons of Abercorn were prominent in the struggle round Derry. Although most supported William of Orange; the 4th Earl of Abercorn supported James II. Trace descent from Claude Hamilton who, in 1583, was created Baron Paisley. Claude's son who, in 1606, was created Earl of Abercorn was the recipient, at the Plantation (1608-1611), of large grants of land in Counties Tyrone and Donegal and, by 1618, he had erected castles and houses at Strabane and Dunnalong.
1091	Hamilton	George	Co. Tyrone	Younger brother of James Hamilton (1090). Served all through the Williamite campaign. Killed in Flanders in 1692.
1092	Hamilton	Colonel Gustavus	Monea Castle, Co. Fermanagh	Grandson of Archibald Hamilton of Cuchonaught, Scotland. Governor of Enniskillen through the actions round the town. Died 1690.
1093	Hamilton	Colonel Gustavus	Manor Hamilton, Co. Leitrim	Son of Sir Frederick Hamilton of Manor Hamilton, Co. Leitrim who was a brother of the 1st Earl of Abercorn. Served all through the Williamite campaign in command of the men of Enniskillen.
1094	Hamilton	Rev. James	Mongeviin Castle, Co. Donegal	Archdeacon of Raphoe. James II stopped here on his way to Derry and sent proposals, through his host Archdeacon Hamilton, of surrender to the garrison.
1095	Hamilton	Rev. Andrew	Kilskeery, Co. Tyrone	Rector of Kilskeery. One of the most prominent of the Enniskillen fighting men.
1096	Hamilton	Sir Frederick (Francis)	Castle Hamilton, Co. Cavan	3rd Baronet of Enderwick, Scotland. Plantation grantees in Co. Cavan.
1097	Hamilton	Francis	Castle Hamilton, Co. Cavan	Son of Sir Frederick Hamilton (1096). Raised a regiment which Sir Frederick and his son brought to Derry.
1098	Hamilton	John	Murvagh, Co. Donegal	Served in Derry with distinction through the siege.
1099	Hamilton	James	Strabane, Co. Tyrone	A leading merchant of Strabane. Prior to the siege he procured powder and supplies from Scotland.
1100	Hamilton	William	Ballyfatton, Co. Tyrone	Grandson of William Hamilton of Priestfield, Scotland who came to Ulster in 1617 and, in 1634, obtained a lease of the lands of Ballyfatton. Served in Derry with distinction through the siege
1101	Hamilton	Captain James	Co. Tyrone	Brother of William Hamilton (1100). Served in Derry through the siege.
1102	Hamilton	Patrick	Dergal, Co. Tyrone	Brother of William Hamilton (1100)
1103	Hamilton	Captain Archibald		
1104	Hamilton	Charles	Co. Tyrone	Brother of William Hamilton (1100). Served in Derry with distinction through the siege.
1105	Hamilton	Robert	Killeloony, Co. Tyrone	Brother of William Hamilton (1100).
1106	Hamilton	Patrick	Co. Tyrone	
1107	Hamilton	Robert	Carrowbeg, Co. Tyrone	
1108	Hamilton	John	Caledon, Co. Tyrone	
1109	Hamilton	Widow Margaret	Co. Tyrone	
1110	Hamilton	James	Cloughmills, Co. Antrim	

Young's ID	Surname	First Name	Residence	Remarks
1111	Hamilton	William	Cloughmills, Co. Antrim	
1112	Hamilton	Captain John	Cloughmills, Co. Antrim	
1113	Hamilton	James	Bangor, Co. Down	Grand-nephew of James Hamilton, subsequently Viscount Clandeboy (son of Rev. Hans Hamilton of Dunlop, Scotland), who secured, in 1605, a large estate from the O'Neills (which was sanctioned by James I) in Co. Down centred on Killyleagh Castle.
1114	Hamilton	James	Tullymore, Co. Down	Grand-nephew of James Hamilton, Viscount Clandeboy (see 1113)
1115	Hamilton	Gawen	Lisivine, Co. Down	Ancestor of Hamiltons of Killyleagh Castle and the Marquess of Dufferin
1116	Hamilton	William	Co. Down	
1117	Hamilton	Patrick	Granskeogh, Co. Down	
1118	Hamilton	John	Erinagh, Co. Down	
1119	Hamilton	James	Carricknasure, Co. Down	
1120	Hamilton	Robert	Co. Down	
1121	Hamilton	Robert	Co. Down	
1122	Hamilton	Archibald	Co. Fermanagh	
1123	Hamilton	James	Co. Fermanagh	
1124	Hamilton	Henry	Co. Cavan	
1125	Hamilton	James	Co. Cavan	
1126	Hamilton	Andrew	Londonderry	Burgess of city of Derry. The Hamiltons were a prominent family in Derry at the time of the siege
1127	Hamilton	Charles	Londonderry	Burgess of city of Derry
1128	Hamilton	William	Londonderry	
1129	Hamilton	John	Londonderry	
1130	Hamilton	John	Londonderry	
1131	Hamilton	Arthur	Londonderry	
1132	Hamilton (or Douglas)	Lord George		Son of Lord William Douglass, Duke of Hamilton and Anne, Duchess of Hamilton. Prominent at the Boyne and subsequent campaign; appointed Colonel of one of the famous Enniskillen regiments in 1691.
1303	Hammersley	George	Co. Monaghan	
1597	Hamond	William	Derry	
556	Hannagh	Lieutenant Andrew		
555	Hannah	Captain		
1484	Harman	Christopher	Co. Cavan	
789	Harper		Derry	
790	Harper	Captain John	Ballymena, Co. Antrim	
791	Harper	Robert	Ballymena, Co. Antrim	
1189	Harrington	Simon	Tyrone	
1221	Harrington	Thomas	Co. Down	
1222	Harrington	William	Co. Down	
1600	Harris	Samuel	Derry	
954	Harrison	Captain Edward	Killultagh, Co. Antrim	Son of Sir Michael Harrison of Ballydargan (died 1664) who settled in Ireland in reign of Charles II. Lived in Old Maghraleave House, near Lisburn. One of 23 gentry of Co. Antrim who raised regiments in defence of Protestant interests in the county. High Sheriff of Co. Antrim in 1678. M.P. for Lisburn from 1692. Died 1703.
955	Harrison	Michael	Killultagh, Co. Antrim	Son of Captain Edward Harrison (954). One of 23 gentry of Co. Antrim who raised regiments in defence of Protestant interests in the county.

Young's ID	Surname	First Name	Residence	Remarks
715	Hart	Captain Henry	Donegal or Londonderry	Son of George Hart of Kildery. Grandson of Captain Henry Hart of Devonshire, an officer in Queen Elizabeth's army who, in 1607, was appointed Governor of Culmore and, at the Plantation, acquired considerable estates in Co. Donegal at Culmore, Muff (Kilderry) and Doe Castle and, in 1613, was appointed an alderman of the city of Derry. He died in 1637 and was buried in St. Columb's Cathedral; his son George Hart of Kilderry married daughter of George Carey of Redcastle and died 1660. Captain Henry Hart died 1712 and his son George, born 1685, married Mariana, heiress of George Vaughan of Buncrana. The Harts were supporters of King William but were not in Derry during siege.
716	Hart	George	Donegal or Londonderry	
717	Hart	George	Donegal or Londonderry	Brother of Captain Henry Hart (715)
718	Hart	Widow Lettice	Co. Cavan	Widow of Merrick Hart of Crobert (or Crovert), Co. Cavan who was a son of Captain Henry Hart, an Elizabethan army officer (see 715).
719	Hart	Thomas	Co. Cavan	Son of Widow Lettice Hart (718)
720	Hart	Major Thomas		
721	Hart	Captain		
722	Hart	Lieutenant		
723	Hart	Captain Morgan	Enniskillen	
724	Hart	Captain George	Enniskillen	
725	Hart	Thomas	Enniskillen	
173	Harvey	John	Derry	
209	Harvey	David	Mintiagh, Co. Donegal	Great grandson of Captain George Harvey of Ickworth who was settled at Dunmore, Co. Donegal by 1620.
210	Harvey	Rev. John	Ballymoney, Co. Antrim	Brother of David Harvey (209)
211	Harvey	Robert	Mintiagh, Co. Donegal	Grandson of Captain George Harvey of Ickworth who was settled at Dunmore, Co. Donegal by 1620
212	Harvey	John	Co. Tyrone	Son of Robert Harvey (211). John Harvey's son George, born 1713, acquired the considerable estate of Malin Head, Co. Donegal
213	Harvey	Sam	Derry	
1018	Hassart	Jason	Co. Fermanagh	
1019	Hassart	Jason junior	Co. Fermanagh	
1020	Hassart	Jason	Mullymesker, near Enniskillen, Co. Fermanagh	Big landowners in the County; between 1852 and 1876, 18,281 acres in Fermanagh belonging to various members of the Hassart family were sold in the Encumbered Estates Court.
1016	Hawkins	Colonel John	Co. Down	Prominent leader in defence of Protestant interests in Co. Down.
1017	Hawkins	Hirom	Co. Armagh	
1598	Hay	Jemmet	Derry	
767	Hayre	James	Co. Tyrone	
768	Hayre	John	Co. Tyrone	
1148	Heardman	William	Londonderry	
617	Henderson	John		
313	Henly	Captain		
1470	Henney	Thomas	Co. Cavan	Yeoman
1471	Henney	Richard	Co. Cavan	Yeoman
423	Herd	Captain Stephen		
424	Herd	Stephen		
425	Herd	James		
314	Herman	Doctor		
536	Heron	Quartermaster Alexander		

Young's ID	Surname	First Name	Residence	Remarks
1522	Herring	John	Derry	
1599	Hibbitts	Margaret	Derry	
40	Hill	William	Hillsborough Castle, Co. Down	The first of the name in Ulster was Sir Moses who came as an officer with the Earl of Essex in 1574 and received considerable grants of land at Hillsborough
280	Hill	Major John	Derry	Son of Samuel Hill, a Cromwellian officer. The Hills of St. Columbs, Derry were descendants.
281	Hill	Captain Jonathan	Derry	Brother of Major John Hill (280)
282	Hillhouse	James	Co. Cavan	
739	Hinderton	Captain Abraham	Coleraine	
1190	Hinderton	John	Tyrone	
551	Hindman	Captain	Derry	Captain of the Derry Guard
552	Hindman	John	Derry	
1304	Hiniston	Thomas	Killiny, Co. Fermanagh	
644	Hobson	Alderman Samuel	Londonderry	Died in 1697
1223	Hodges	Mark	Co. Down	
980	Hogg	Alexander	Lough Eske, Co. Donegal	
981	Hogg	William	Co. Down	
983	Hogg	Robert		
619	Holding	Mrs Susannah		Described as 'a gentlewoman of eighty years old' in Thomas Ash's Diary.
1408	Holland	James	Co. Monaghan	
1409	Holland	John	Co. Monaghan	
1472	Holland	Roger	Co. Cavan	Yeoman
462	Holmes	Captain Nicholas		
463	Holmes	George	Coleraine	
464	Holmes	Thomas	Co. Monaghan	
465	Homes	John	Derry	
1558	Hookes	Povey	Enniskillen	
21	Hopkins	Bishop Ezekiel	Derry	Bishop of Derry 1685 to 1690
770	Hoult	John	Derry	
771	Hoult	Ralph		
454	Houston	James	Garveleigh, Castlederg	
455	Houston	Robert		
456	Houston	John		
941	Houston	Colonel Robert	Craigs, Co. Antrim	The Houstons settled in Co. Antrim from Scotland early in the 17th century and purchased the estate of Craigs
942	Houston	Francis	Craigs, Co. Antrim	
1074	Houston	Rev. David		Presbyterian minister who came over to Ulster about 1688.
1556	Howell	Henry	Enniskillen	
1305	Hudson	Daniel	Co. Cavan	Came to Enniskillen as a refugee in spring of 1689, fought alongside the men of Enniskillen and subsequently settled in the town.
1306	Hudson	Robert	Co. Tyrone	
1358	Huelt	John	Co. Armagh	
1359	Huelt	Nathaniel	Co. Armagh	
1149	Hueson	John	Ballyshannon, Donegal	
1150	Hueson	Michael	Ballyshannon, Donegal	
982	Huey	Captain James	Muff, Londonderry	
580	Hughes	Quartermaster John		
1565	Hughs	Edward	Enniskillen	Lieutenant in local force
1566	Hughs	Thomas	Enniskillen	

Young's ID	Surname	First Name	Residence	Remarks
120	Hume	Sir John	Castle Hume, Co. Fermanagh	Grandson of Sir John Hume of Berwickshire, Scotland who was a grantee at the Plantation of Castle Hume estate in Fermanagh
122	Hume	George	Enniskillen, Co. Fermanagh	
123	Hume	James	Knockballemore, Co. Fermanagh	Nephew of Sir Gustavus Hume (121)
124	Hume	Rev. George	Tully, Co. Fermanagh	
125	Hume	Thomas	Cavan	
121	Hume	Sir Gustavus	Castle Hume, Co. Fermanagh	Son of Sir John Hume (120)
254	Humfrey		Cavanacor, Co. Donegal	The Humfrey family settled in Wicklow in 1655. Married into Keys family of Cavanacor in 1823.
255	Humphrey	Thomas	Co. Cavan	
256	Humphrey	John	Co. Fermanagh	
257	Humphrey	Thomas	Co. Fermanagh	
258	Humphrey	William	Co. Fermanagh	
815	Hunt	Samuel	Derry	
816	Hunt	Francis	Derry	One of 13 apprentice boys who shut the gates on 7 December 1688
819	Hunter	Captain Henry	Londonderry	His diary of the siege was published in 1841
820	Hunter	Margaret	Derry	
821	Hunter	John	Derry	
899	Irwin	Alexander		
900	Irwin	Edward	Derry	One of 13 apprentice boys who shut the gates on 7 December 1688.
901	Irwin	Archibald	Timpain, Co. Tyrone	
902	Irwin	John	Mullinboy, Co. Londonderry	
903	Irwin	William	Ballydullagh, Co. Fermanagh	Also known as William Irvine, brother of Sir Gerard Irvine (see 906). Succeeded to Castle Irvine estate on death of Sir Gerard Irvine in 1689.
904	Irwin	Christopher	Ballydullagh, Co. Fermanagh	Son of William Irwin (903). Succeeded his father, who died 1714, to Castle Irvine estate.
905	Irwin	James	Co. Down	
1513	Islen	Richard	Derry	
1602	Jack	Jennett	Derry	
140	Jackson	Ensign Thomas	Drumballyhagan Clark, Tobermore, Co. Der	The Jacksons from Westmorland, England came to Ulster in Charles I's reign. Thomas Jackson, c. 1639, acquired lands in Coleraine and built Jackson Hall.
141	Jackson	Ensign Richard		
142	Jackson	Mabel	Derry	
143	Jackson	Edward	Co. Down	
1410	James	Henry	Co. Monaghan	
798	Jemmet	Warham	Derry	
1601	Jenkins	Helinor	Derry	Tax collector
266	Jennings (or Jenny)	Frances	Derry	
265	Jenny	Captain Rev. Christopher	Ardboe and Ardtrea, Co. Tyrone	Rector of Ardboe and Ardtrea
61	Johnson	Squire Richard	Glasslough, Co. Monaghan	The Scottish Border family of Johnson settled in considerable numbers in Fermanagh, Monaghan and Armagh in the first half of 17th century
62	Johnston	Baptist	Co. Monaghan	
63	Johnston	William	Co. Monaghan	
64	Johnston	Alexander	Co. Monaghan	
65	Johnston	Captain John	Drumconnell, Co. Armagh	Brother of William Johnston (63)
66	Johnston	Captain Joseph	Co. Monaghan	
67	Johnston	Walter	Mellick, Co. Fermanagh	
68	Johnston	Francis	Derrycholaght, Co. Fermanagh	High Sheriff of County Fermanagh in 1678
69	Johnston	James	Co. Fermanagh	Son of Walter Johnston (67)
70	Johnston	Francis	Monaghan	Son of Francis Johnston (68)

Young's ID	Surname	First Name	Residence	Remarks
71	Johnston	George	Co. Down	
72	Johnston	Hugh	Rademon, Co. Down	
73	Johnston	Thomas	Co. Down	
74	Johnston	Andrew	Co. Fermanagh	
75	Johnston	Robert	Aghamee, Co. Fermanagh	
76	Johnston	Robert	Co. Fermanagh	
77	Johnston	Thomas	Co. Monaghan	
78	Johnston	James	Co. Monaghan	
79	Johnston	William	Co. Monaghan	
80	Johnston	Archibald	Co. Armagh	
81	Johnston	Henry		
82	Johnston	Thomas		
83	Johnston	Joseph		
84	Johnston	George	Glynn, Co. Antrim	
85	Johnston	Charles	Glynn, Co. Antrim	
379	Johnston	Rev.		
1360	Jones	John	Co. Armagh	
1361	Jones	Thomas	Derry	
1362	Jones	Mary	Derry	
1151	Jordan	Patrick	Castleroe, Donegal	
535	Kane	Lieutenant Richard		Descended from O'Kane of Keenaght, one of his forebears settled at Carrickfergus and acquired large estate at Duneane, Co. Antrim
1411	Karnoghan	David	Co. Monaghan	
1473	Keep	Richard	Co. Cavan	Yeoman
457	Kelso	Rev. John	Enniskillen	Presbyterian minister of Enniskillen. Died shortly after relief of Derry
788	Kem	Councillor	Derry	
1485	Kempson	Grace	Co. Cavan	
624	Kennedy	Horace	Derry	Sheriff of the city in 1688. Mayor of Derry in 1698.
625	Kennedy	Captain John		Fought with gallantry at Pennyburn on 25 April and at Butcher's Gate on 28 June 1689.
626	Kennedy	David		The Kennedy family have had a long association with the city
243	Kerr	Lieutenant James	Grasskeogh, Rossory Parish, Co. Fermanagh	
244	Kerr	John	Co. Fermanagh	
245	Kerr	Robert	Omagh, Co. Tyrone	
246	Kerr	Thomas	Omagh, Co. Tyrone	
247	Kerr	Thomas	Co. Tyrone	
1412	Keyran	William	Co. Monaghan	
252	Keys	Captain Thomas	Cavanacor, Co. Donegal	
253	Keys	Frederick	Cavanacor, Co. Donegal	Brother of Captain Thomas Keys (252). Tradition that King James dined at Cavanacor on his way to Derry.
1554	Kilte	William	Enniskillen	
32	King	Robert	Boyle Abbey, Co. Roscommon	2nd Baron Kingston. First of the family in Ireland was John King who received large grants of land during Queen Elizabeth's reign
33	King	John	Boyle Abbey, Co. Roscommon	3rd Baron Kingston. He married daughter of Florence O'Kane, of the ancient family of Keenaght, Limavady, in 1683.
967	King	Robert	Enniskillen	
968	King	Captain Francis	Enniskillen	
1545	King	James	Enniskillen	
1546	King	Charles	Enniskillen	Cornet of horse
1152	Kingsmill	John	Donegal	

Young's ID	Surname	First Name	Residence	Remarks
334	Kinnaston	Captain Charles		
308	Kirke	Major-General John Percy		Garrison commander with 20 years experience in Tangier. In command of a fleet of 30 ships that relieved Derry. Killed at Athlone in 1691.
1413	Knelson	John	Co. Monaghan	
1414	Knight	George	Co. Monaghan	
1415	Knight	Abraham	Co. Monaghan	
1603	Knobbs	Jean	Derry	
368	Knox	Captain Rev. John	Glasslough, Co. Monaghan	Rector of Glasslough, Diocese of Clogher
909	Knox	Thomas	Belfast	In 1692 purchased an estate at Dungannon, Co. Tyrone; from whom descend the Earls of Ranfurly, Dungannon. The Knoxes derived the title of Ranfurly from their Scottish estate of Ranphorlie.
910	Knox	John	Glasslough, Co. Monaghan	
911	Knox	John	Raphoe, Donegal or Londonderry	
912	Knox	William	Raphoe, Donegal or Londonderry	
913	Knox	Andrew	Donegal or Londonderry	Descended from Andrew Knox, Bishop of the Isles in Scotland who from 1611 until his death in 1632 was Bishop of Raphoe, Co. Donegal. Related to Knox of Ranfurly, Scotland and ancestor of Knox family of Prehen, Derry.
914	Knox	Alexander		
915	Knox	James		
916	Knox	James	Ballyvennox, near Limavady, Co. Derry	Tenant farmer of some 100 acres in townland of Ballyvennox
917	Knox	Robert	Murder Hole Road between Coleraine and Limavady	Owner of mountain farm on side of road between Coleraine and Limavady known as the murder hole.
1456	Lacken	John	Co. Monaghan	Yeoman
262	Lance	Colonel Thomas	Coleraine	Commander of the Coleraine regiment in the siege of Derry. Died 11 September 1689 in the city, where he was buried.
884	Lane	Captain Thomas		Served with distinction through the siege. This family long settled in Co. Derry. William Lane of Coleraine, who died 1725, was agent of the Irish Society.
885	Lane	Henry		
886	Lane	Anne	Derry	
1023	Lanesborough	Dowager Viscountess		The first of the name in Ireland was Sir George Lane, Secretary for Ireland, who acquired the estate of Tulske, Co. Roscommon, and was created Viscount Lanesborough in 1676.
1024	Lanesborough	2nd Viscount		Son of Dowager Viscountess Lanesborough (1023) and Sir George Lane
449	Langford	Sir Arthur	Summer Hill, Co. Meath	The Langfords were closely connected with the town of Carrickfergus, Co. Antrim as two brothers, Sir Roger and Sir Hercules Langford, were captains in the services of Elizabeth and James I at Carrickfergus.
1652	Lanier	General Sir John	England	Commander of the 1st Dragoon Guards at the Boyne. Killed at Steinkirk, in William's Flanders campaign, in 1692
1606	Latey	John	Derry	
707	Laundell	John		
1224	Law	Cornet John	Co. Down	Received freedom of the city on 15 January 1691
461	Lawder	John	Enniskillen	Son of William Lawder of Drumaleague, Co. Leitrim
345	Leake	Captain		Captain of HMS Dartmouth which accompanied the three merchant ships carrying provisions - Mountjoy, Phoenix and Jerusalem - in the Breaking of the Boom
1153	Leatham	Captain William	Donegal, Londonderry	Grandson of William Leathem, Recorder of Derry
101	Lecky	Captain Alexander	Londonderry	Sheriff of city of Londonderry in 1677. Mayor of the city in 1691 & 1695. Died 1717. Buried in St. Columb's Cathedral.
1191	Lee	Samuel	Tyrone	
1192	Leech	Thomas	Ballore, Tyrone	

Young's ID	Surname	First Name	Residence	Remarks
1193	Leech	William	Ballore, Tyrone	
1416	Legate	Patrick	Co. Monaghan	
278	Leighton	Captain Baldwin	Hillsborough Castle, Co. Down	Brother of Edward Leighton, a Shropshire landlord
153	Lenox	James	Londonderry	Son of James Lenox who settled in the city in early half of 17th century. Mayor of Derry 1693 & 1697. Died 1723 and buried in St. Columb's Cathedral. Grandson, Clotworthy Lenox married, in 1745, Alicia, heiress of George Conyngham of Springhill, Moneymore, Co. Derry.
1487	Leods	Michael	Co. Cavan	
1307	Leonard	John	Maguiresbridge, Co. Fermanagh	
110	Leslie	William	Prospect, now Leslie Hill, Ballymoney, Co. A	The first of this Scottish house to come to Antrim was William's father, Henry Leslie, a grandson of 4th Earl of Rothes.
111	Leslie	James	Sheeplands	Brother of William Leslie (110).
1073	Leslie	Rev. Charles	Donegal or Londonderry	Episcopalian minister. Son of John Leslie of Wardis, Scotland who was consecrated Bishop of Clogher in 1661. He inherited the Bishop's Glasslough estate, Co. Monaghan in 1672.
1075	Leslie	Rev. Dr. John	Co. Fermanagh	Probably same person as 1075 with estates in both Fermanagh and Leitrim
1076	Leslie	Rev. Dr. John	Co. Leitrim	
1077	Leslie	John	Co. Tyrone	Son of the rector of Urney, Co. Tyrone. Died leading a cavalry charge at Aughrim
1078	Leslie	William	Co. Monaghan	
1607	Letey	Katherine	Derry	
1540	Letournell	Thomas	Enniskillen	A Huguenot settler in Enniskillen. Prominent in defence. Provost of Enniskillen in 1694 and 1702
1486	Lewis	Richard	Co. Cavan	
351	Lindsay	Robert	Loughrey, Co. Tyrone	The first of the family, Robert Lindsay settled at Loughrey in 1611
352	Lindsay	Alexander	Cahoo, Co. Tyrone	Surgeon and brother of Robert Lindsay (351). Killed by falling bombs on 5 June 1689
353	Lindsay	Andrew	Donegal or Londonderry	
355	Lindsay	George I.	Derry	
356	Lindsay	Matthew	Enniskillen	
1608	Linegar	Patrick	Derry	
646	Linn	John		
354	Linzy (or Lindsay)	Sergeant James		
272	Lisburne	The Dowager Viscountess		Mother of Adam Loftus (271)
1605	Lithgoe	Robert	Derry	
1604	Lithgom	David	Derry	
1308	Little	William	Drumenagh, Co. Fermanagh	
966	Lloyd	Colonel Thomas	Croghan, Co. Roscommon	One of the prominent leaders of the men of Enniskillen, gaining the nickname 'the little Cromwell'. Grandson of Thomas Lloyd of Wales who settled in Co. Leitrim early in the 17th century and son of Captain Owen Lloyd, M.P. for Boyle in 1661, who acquired the estate at Croghan.
1225	Lock	Anthony	Co. Down	
271	Loftus	Adam		2nd Viscount Lisburne. Descendant of 16th century Adam Loftus, Archbishop of Dublin
793	Logan	John		
794	Logan	Alexander	Derry	
1417	Logher	John	Co. Monaghan	
618	Long	Lieutenant Henry	Derry	Burgess in Derry Corporation.
1457	Loughey	John	Co. Monaghan	Yeoman
1458	Loughey	Patrick	Co. Monaghan	Yeoman

Young's ID	Surname	First Name	Residence	Remarks
458	Louther	Lieutenant Robert	Co. Armagh	
1363	Lovell	John		Died during siege. Son of James Lowry who came from Scotland to Tyrone early in the 17th century and died in 1665.
285	Lowry	John	Ahenis, Co. Tyrone	
286	Lowry	Jane	Ahenis, Co. Tyrone	Daughter of William Hamilton of Ballyfatton and wife of John Lowry (285)
287	Lowry	John	Ahenis, Co. Tyrone	Son of John Lowry (285). Died 1698
288	Lowry	Humphrey	Derry	
459	Lowther	Lancelot	Co. Leitrim	
460	Lowther	William	Co. Leitrim	
1364	Loyd	Charles	Co. Armagh	
1538	Lucy	James	Enniskillen	
1418	Lundsell	Alexander	Co. Monaghan	
1	Lundy	Lieutenant-Colonel Robert	Scotland	Governor of Derry, December 1688 to 20 April 1689
978	Lyndon	Captain John	Carrickfergus, Co. Antrim	Son of Sir John Lyndon of Carrickfergus
645	Lynn	Sergeant		Killed in last sortie of 17 July 1689
117	Macartney	Captain George	Belfast, Co. Antrim	Descended from Macartney of Auchinleck, Scotland. Settled in Co. Antrim in 1649. High Sheriff of County Antrim in 1678 & 1688
118	Macartney	James	Auchinleck, Scotland	Son of Captain George Macartney (117)
118	Macartney	George	Belfast	Son of Captain George Macartney (117). Leading merchant in Belfast. Purchased Lissanoure castle, Co. Antrim from the O'Haras in 1733.
119	Macartney	Arthur	Co. Antrim	May be a younger son of Captain George Macartney (117) or descendant of George Macartney of Blacket, Scotland who settled near town of Antrim about 1630
829	Mackay	Lieutenant		Killed in Pennyburn sortie of 21 April 1689
830	Mackay	John	Multo, Co. Antrim	
1651	Mackay	General Andrew	Scotland	As a commander in King William's Irish army, from 1690, he served with distinction at Athlone, Aughrim and Limerick. Killed at Steinkirk, in William's Flanders campaign, in 1692
832	Mackee	Jannett	Derry	
12	Mackenzie	Rev. John	Derryloran, Cookstown, Co. Tyrone	Presbyterian minister. Published his 'History of the Siege' in 1690.
827	Mackey	Lieutenant William	Londonderry or Donegal	
826	Mackie	Ensign William		
828	Mackie	Lieutenant		
831	Macky	Josiah	Derry	
1255	Maclure	James	Co. Antrim	
103	Macnaghten	Mrs Helen	Benvarden, Co. Antrim	John Macnaghten of Benvarden married Helen Stafford of Mount Stafford
104	Macnaghten	Edmund	Beardiville, Co. Antrim	Son of John Macnaghten and Helen Stafford
1155	Madden	Daniel	Londonderry	
1311	Maddson	Lieutenant Edward	Arny, Co. Monaghan	
1312	Maddson	Cornet John	Arny, Co. Monaghan	
1313	Maddson	John	Clonegally, Co. Fermanagh	
665	Maghlin	Captain John		
666	Maghlin	Robert		
667	Maghlin	Lieutenant		
46	Magill	Sir John	Gillhall, Co. Down	
47	Magill	Captain James	Gillhall, Co. Down	Son of Sir John Magill (46). On retreat to Derry he was killed at Portglenone attempting to prevent General Richard Hamilton's passage of the Bann.
48	Magill	Captain Hugh	Kerstown	Son of Sir John Magill (46).
49	Magill	John	Mienallan, Co. Down	Son of Sir John Magill (46).
50	Magill	William	Gillhall, Co. Down	Son of Captain James Magill (47)

Young's ID	Surname	First Name	Residence	Remarks
51	Magill	John	Tullycarn, Co. Down	
52	Magill	Captain Hugh	Co. Fermanagh	
1618	Man	John	Derry	
898	Mansfield	Ralph	Killygordon, Co. Donegal	Grandson of Ralph Mansfield, a grantee at the Plantation of 1000 acres which became the manor of Killygordon, near Stranorlar.
1501	Mansly	Captain	Co. Leitrim	
671	Manson	Captain Thomas		
672	Manson	Theophilus		
673	Manson	James		
674	Manson	William		
675	Manson	William	Co. Down	
1650	Marlborough	Duke of	England	John Churchill, a General in James II's army, defected to King William in 1689. Joined the Irish campaign, with 5000 men, in Autumn 1690, and captured the Irish strongholds of Cork and Kinsale. He was created Duke of Marlborough in 1702. The family home of the Dukes of Marlborough at Blenheim Palace, Oxfordshire was completed in 1722.
1620	Marshall	John	Derry	
979	Mathews	Rev. Lemuel	Hillsborough or Annahilt	Archdeacon of Down
1567	Mathews	James	Enniskillen	
39	Maxwell	Sir George	Killyleagh Castle, Co. Down	Son of Sir Robert Maxwell of Waringstown
847	Maxwell	William	Derry	
848	Maxwell	Thomas	Derry	Killed by cannon on 4 June 1689
849	Maxwell	Captain		
850	Maxwell	Anne	Londonderry or Donegal	Sister of Governor George Walker who married William Maxwell of Falkland, Co. Monaghan
851	Maxwell	James		
852	Maxwell	Robert	Farnham, Co. Cavan	The first of the family in Ulster was Rev. Robert Maxwell, son of Sir Robert Maxwell of Calderwood, Scotland who came over late in Queen Elizabeth's reign and became Dean of Armagh.
853	Maxwell	John	Farnham, Co. Cavan	
854	Maxwell	Arthur	Drumbridge, Co. Down	
855	Maxwell	George	Derryboy, Co. Down	
856	Maxwell	Hugh	Ballyquintan, Co. Down	
857	Maxwell	Henry	Glenarb, Co. Tyrone	
858	Maxwell	James	Glenarb, Co. Tyrone	
859	Maxwell	Thomas	Strabane, Co. Tyrone	
860	Maxwell	Rev. James	Co. Leitrim	
861	Maxwell	William	Falkland, Co. Monaghan	
862	Maxwell	James	Co. Armagh	
1367	May	Richard	Co. Armagh	
1368	Mayo	Algernon	Co. Armagh	
1616	McCaffer	Katherine	Derry	
1617	McCamus	Jean	Derry	
1365	McCaul	John	Co. Armagh	
283	McCausland	Captain Oliver	Strabane	Cousin of Colonel Robert McCausland, died 1734, of Fruit Hill (Drenagh), Limavady, the first of the family living there, who had property near Cappagh, Co. Tyrone. Descended from John MacAuslane who acquired the lands of Buchanan on the Lennox, Scotland.
284	McCausland	Andrew	Clanaghmore, Co. Tyrone	Relative of Colonel Robert McCausland, died 1734, of Fruit Hill (Drenagh), the first of the family living there, who had property near Cappagh, Co. Tyrone

Young's ID	Surname	First Name	Residence	Remarks
647	McClelland	Mathew		
648	McClelland	John		
365	McClenaghan	Rev. Michael	Derry	Rector of Derry
1194	McClenaghan	Andrew	Tyrone	
1195	McClenaghan	David	Tyrone	
363	McCollum	Alexander		Emigrated in 1718 and settled at Londonderry, New Hampshire
1527	McConnell	Robert	Enniskillen	
651	McCormac	William	Co. Down	
652	McCormac	Captain William	Enniskillen	Served with distinction in defence of Enniskillen
650	McCormick	Captain James	Lisburn	Served with distinction through siege.
1615	McCrea	Ann	Derry	
1309	McCreery	Robert	Co. Tyrone	
530	McCullagh	Captain Henry	The Grange, Co. Antrim	
531	McCullagh	Captain Archibald	The Grange, Co. Antrim	Secured the bridge across the Bann at Coleraine to enable withdrawal of Coleraine garrison to Derry
532	McCullagh	Lieutenant John	The Grange, Co. Antrim	
533	McCullagh	Ensign William	The Grange, Co. Antrim	
534	McCullagh	Lieutenant Anthony	The Grange, Co. Antrim	
1520	McCustion	Dan	Derry	
1611	McCutcheon	John	Derry	
1610	McDowell	An	Derry	
1310	McFadden	Charles	Cavan	
330	McFetrick	William	Carnglass, Co. Antrim	
1609	McGee	Mary	Derry	Messenger of the garrison who swam down the river with intelligence for relief fleet. Captured
712	McGimpsey			
1419	McGirby	James	Co. Monaghan	
360	McGregor	Rev. James	Magilligan, Co. Derry	Son of Captain McGregor and founder of Londonderry, New Hampshire
1612	McKain	Joshea	Derry	
1613	McKerragh	David	Derry	
362	McKien	James	Ballymoney, Co. Antrim	Emigrated in 1718 and settled at Londonderry, New Hampshire
1614	McLaughlin	John	Derry	
1154	McLornane	Captain Mathew	Donegal or Derry	
1226	McNab	John	Co. Down	
1420	McNab	Andrew	Co. Monaghan	
525	McNeale	Daniel	Dundrum, Co. Down	
526	McNeale	Rev. Archibald	Downpatrick, Co. Down	
527	McNeale	Rev. Dean John	Downpatrick, Co. Down	Dean of Down. Son of Rev. Daniel McNeale, rector of Billy parish, Co. Antrim
528	McNeale	John	Billy, Co. Antrim	Descended from family settled at Currysheskin, Billy, Co. Antrim for many generations
529	McNeale	Captain Hugh	Clare, Co. Antrim	The McNeales were among the original grantees of estates on the land of 1st Earl of Antrim
329	McPhedris	Lieutenant		Killed in the Pennyburn Mill sortie of 21 April 1689
1488	McVise	Thomas	Co. Cavan	
1422	Mead	David	Co. Monaghan	
1315	Means	John	Stranaragh, Co. Fermanagh	
1491	Mee	John	Co. Cavan	
1619	Mercer	Peter	Derry	
1369	Meredith	William	Co. Armagh	
1316	Merrick	Richard	Magherastephenagh, Co. Fermanagh	

Young's ID	Surname	First Name	Residence	Remarks
1317	Merrick	Hugh	Co. Armagh	
199	Mervyn	Audley	Trillick, Omagh, Co. Tyrone	The Mervyns settled at Trillick on invitation of their relatives the Touchets (Baron Audley) of Forthill, Wiltshire, England who, in 1615, secured large grants of land round Omagh.
200	Mervyn	Henry	Omagh, Co. Tyrone	
201	Mervyn	George	Co. Tyrone	
842	Middleton	Captain	Co. Armagh	
923	Miller	Captain Stephen	Donegal or Londonderry	Died at Kilrea in 1729
924	Miller	Margaret	Derry	
1423	Mills	John	Co. Monaghan	
7	Mitchelburn	Colonel John		Governor of Derry from 30 June 1689. Died 1721. Buried at Old Glendermot Graveyard. Grandson of Sir Richard Mitchelburn of Broadhurst, Sussex
348	Mitchell	Lietenant David		
349	Mitchell	Alexander		
350	Mitchell	John		
1534	Mitchell	James	Enniskillen	
1318	Moffet	John	Letterboy, Co. Fermanagh	
327	Mogridge	John	Derry	Secretary to the Corporation of Derry
328	Mogridge	James	Derry	
653	Moncrieff	Captain Thomas	Derry	Prominent Alderman of the city. Mayor of Derry in 1678, 1679, 1680, 1701 and 1728
392	Monroe	Colonel Henry	Co. Down	Killed before Limerick in 1691
26	Montgomery	Hugh	Mount Alexander, Co. Down	2nd Earl of Mount Alexander. Great grandson of Sir Hugh Montgomery, 6th Laird of Braidstone, who, in 1605, secured large grants of land from the Crown in the Ards, Co. Down and became Viscount Montgomery of the Ards.
177	Montgomery	William	Rosemount, Greyabbey, Co. Down	Born at Aughantain, Co. Tyrone in 1633 and author of the Montgomery Manuscripts. Grandson of Sir Hugh, 1st Viscount Montgomery of the Ards.
178	Montgomery	James	Rosemount, Greyabbey, Co. Down	Son of William Montgomery (177)
179	Montgomery	Robert	Rosemount, Greyabbey, Co. Down	
180	Montgomery	Cornet William	Gransheogh, Co. Down and Maghera, Co. [Derry	Great grandson of John Montgomery (a kinsman of Sir Hugh Montgomery of Braidstone, Scotland who settled in the Ards, Co. Down in 1605) who was given the townland of Gransheogh (or Granyshaw). The family also acquired churchlands at Maghera, Co. Derry from another relation George Montgomery, Bishop of Derry
181	Montgomery	Hugh	Ballymagowan, Co. Down	Son of Rev James Montgomery of Hazelhead, Scotland who came to Co. Down about 1640
182	Montgomery	John	Creboy, Co. Down	Great grandson of Patrick Montgomery of Blackhouse, Scotland who was granted Creboy by his kinsman Sir Hugh Montgomery in 1629
183	Montgomery	Hugh	Ballymacclady, Co. Down	Another branch of the Braidstone Montgomerys
184	Montgomery	Colonel Hugh	Ballylesson, Co. Down	Great grandson of 1st Viscount Montgomery of the Ards
185	Montgomery	Robert	Derryburke, Co. Frmanagh	George Montgomery, as Bishop of Derry and Clogher from 1618, settled kinsman Hugh Montgomery (grandfather of Robert) on churchlands at Derryburke, near Enniskillen
186	Montgomery	Rev. Andrew	Ballymore, Carrickmacross, Co. Monaghan	Rector of Ballymore. Brother of Robert Montgomery (185)
187	Montgomery	John	Croghan, Co. Donegal	George Montgomery, as Bishop of Derry, settled kinsman Rev. Alexander Montgomery of Hazelhead, Scotland (grandfather of John) on churchlands at Castle Doe, Donegal.
188	Montgomery	Hugh	Co. Monaghan	
189	Montgomery	Captain Hugh	Co. Leitrim	
190	Montgomery	William	Derry	

Young's ID	Surname	First Name	Residence	Remarks
214	Montgomery	Hugh	Benvarden, Co. Antrim	Only connected to the Siege by marriage to daughters of defenders. This branch of the Montgomerys of Ayrshire were based in Glenarm from mid-17th century and purchased the Benvarden estate at end of 18th century.
773	Montgomery	John		
774	Montgomery	John		
775	Montgomery	John	Derry	
86	Moore	Squire William	Aughnacloy, Co. Tyrone	Aughnacloy is the central town of the district, where the Moores held 2 large estates of Dromont and Garvey
87	Moore	Colonel William	Dromont, Co. Tyrone	
88	Moore	Captain William	Augher, Co. Tyrone	
89	Moore	James Montgomery	Garvey, Co. Tyrone	Sheriff of Tyrone in 1697
90	Moore	James Montgomery	Garvey, Co. Tyrone	Son of James Montgomery Moore (89). Sheriff of Tyrone in 1701
91	Moore	John	Co. Tyrone	
92	Moore	John	Co. Tyrone	
93	Moore	Thomas	Co. Tyrone	
94	Moore	James	Garvagh, Co. Cavan	
95	Moore	James	Co. Monaghan	
96	Moore	Patrick	Derry	
97	Moore	Joseph	Derry	
98	Moore	Robert	Enniskillen	
99	Moore	John	Derry	
100	Moore	William	Derry	The Moores (or Muirs) were of an old Galloway stock who settled in Counties Tyrone, Cavan and Monaghan in early days of the Plantation.
1156	Moore	Randall	Donegal or Derry	
1227	Moore	James senior	Co. Down	
1228	Moore	James junior	Co. Down	
1366	Moore	James	Co. Armagh	
1421	Moorecroft	William	Co. Monaghan	
371	Morgan	Rev. Robert	Cappagh, Co. Tyrone	Curate of Cappagh, Diocese of Armagh
1196	Morris	Rev. John	Tyrone	
581	Morris	Ensign John		
364	Morrison	John		Emigrated in 1718 and settled at Londonderry, New Hampshire
655	Morrison	Lieutenant Robert		One of 13 apprentice boys who shut the gates on 7 December 1688.
656	Morrison	James		
657	Morrison	Theophilus		
658	Morrison	William		
659	Morrison	Robert		
660	Morrison	Elizabeth		
661	Morrison	Henry		
662	Morrison	William		Elected Burgess of Derry Corporation in September 1689 in recognition of siege service
663	Morrison	Adam	Coolgarry, Co. Tyrone	
1489	Mortimer	Charles	Co. Cavan	
1490	Mortimer	James	Co. Cavan	
1314	Morton	Edward	Mullinagough, Co. Fermanagh	
1198	Moss	Rev. Richard	Tyrone	
1197	Mounteith	Joseph	Tyrone	
202	Moutray	James	Favour Royal, Co. Tyrone	Grandson of Robert Moutray, 9th Laird of Seafield, Fifeshire. The Moutrays acquired Favour Royal estate, owned by the Erskines, by marriage.
520	Mulholland	Captain	Eden, Maghera, Co. Derry	

Young's ID	Surname	First Name	Residence	Remarks
521	Mulholland	Bernard	Eden, Maghera, Co. Derry	
522	Mulholland	David	Eden, Maghera, Co. Derry	
523	Mulholland	John	Eden, Maghera, Co. Derry	
969	Mulloy	Lieutenant Toby	Enniskillen	
323	Murdach	Quartermaster		
411	Murray	Colonel Adam	Ling, Cumber Upper, Co. Derry	Grandson of Gideon Murray of Philiphaugh, Scotland who settled at Ling in 1648. Adam Murray was the garrison's military leader and 'driving force in all the garrison's sorties'. Died 1706. Buried in Old Glendermot graveyard
412	Murray	Captain James	Ling, Cumber Upper, Co. Derry	Son of Colonel Adam Murray (411)
413	Murray	James		
414	Murray	Captain Sam		
415	Murray	Henry		
984	Mussenden	Jeremy	Hillsborough, Co. Down	Acquired the estate of Larchfield near Hillsborough before 1688.
796	Neely	Sergeant		
797	Neely	John	Co. Tyrone	
1370	Nelthorpe	Edward	Co. Armagh	
1541	Neper	Jo	Enniskillen	
807	Nesbitt	Alexander	Tullydonnell, Co. Donegal	This family settled in the county in early Plantation times
808	Nesbitt	James	Tullydonnell, Co. Donegal	
809	Nesbitt	John	Tullydonnell, Co. Donegal	
810	Nesbitt	James	Killygreen, Co. Tyrone	
811	Nesbitt	Prudence	Tullydonnell, Co. Donegal	Wife of John Nesbitt (809)
812	Nesbitt	Captain Andrew		
813	Nesbitt	Lieutenant Albert		
814	Nesbitt	Cornet James		
1459	Netters	Thomas	Co. Cavan	Yeoman
333	Nevil	Captain Francis	Co. Cavan	Compiler of map of Derry at time of the siege
1492	Newborough	Broghill	Co. Cavan	
1493	Newborough	Thomas		
593	Newcomen	Sir Thomas	Kenagh, Co. Longford	Killed at Enniskillen in 1689
594	Newcomen	George	Kenagh, Co. Longford	Son of Sir Thomas Newcomen (593). Fought at the Boyne and killed before Limerick
595	Newcomen	Captain Thomas	Kenagh, Co. Longford	Son of Sir Thomas Newcomen (593). Fought at the Boyne where he lost a hand.
596	Newcomen	Beverley	Kenagh, Co. Longford	Son of Sir Thomas Newcomen (593). Fought at the Boyne.
597	Newcomen	Captain Charles	Kenagh, Co. Longford	Son of Sir Thomas Newcomen (593). Served with Enniskillen Dragoons
1559	Newstead	Richard	Enniskillen	
992	Newton	N.W.	Derry	
991	Newtoun	Lieutenant William	Londonderry	William Newton was Sheriff of Derry in 1686 and 1687
1502	Nicholls	Gustavus	Co. Leitrim	
1503	Nicholls	William	Co. Leitrim	
1504	Nicholson	Captain Edward	Co. Leitrim	
1622	Nivine	William	Derry	
1623	Nivine	Robert	Derry	
1624	Nivine	Samuel	Derry	
53	Noble	Major Arthur	Derryree, Lisnaskea, Co. Fermanagh	The family settled in Fermanagh, from Cornwall, early in the 17th century
215	Norman	Alderman Samuel	Derry	Mayor of Derry in 1672. Died 1692 and buried in St. Columb's Cathedral
1229	Norris	John	Co. Down	
1621	Nutt	Andrew	Derry	
1371	Obins	Anthony	Co. Armagh	

Young's ID	Surname	First Name	Residence	Remarks
1372	Obins	Hanslett	Co. Armagh	
447	Obre	Captain Francis	Lisburn	Son of Francis Obre of Cantilew, Co. Armagh; the Obre family acquired property there by marriage in 1632.
1625	O'Brien	Roger	Derry	
1649	O'Brien	William, 7th Baron of Inchiquin	Dromoland Castle, Co. Clare	Unlike other members of his family he was a strong supporter of King William. The O'Briens trace their descent from Brian Boru, High King of Ireland 1002 to 1014. In 1543 Murrough O'Brien, Prince of Thomond in the Gaelic nobility, was created Baron Inichiquin on condition that he submitted to English law and culture and converted to the Protestant faith.
1647	Ormonde	James, 12th Earl	Kilkenny Castle	12th Earl of Ormonde. Anglo-Irish Protestant and leading agent of royal authority in Ireland until his death in 1688. The founder of the great house of Ormonde was Theobald Fitzwalter (whose successors adopted the surname Butler), one of the Anglo-Norman Barons who came to Ireland, in 1169, with Strongbow, i.e. Richard, son of Gilbert de Clare, 1st Earl of Pembroke. Strongbow became King of Leinster in 1171.
1648	Ormonde	James, 13th Earl	Kilkenny Castle	Grandson of James, 12th Earl of Ormonde (1647). Officer in King William's army and fought at the Battle of the Boyne.
1157	Orr	John	Letterkenny, Donegal	
1158	Orr	James	Letterkenny, Donegal	
387	Osborne	Rev. Alexander	Dublin	Presbyterian minister of Brigh, Co. Tyrone before becoming minister in Dublin just prior to the 1688 revolution
388	Osborne	Thomas	Enniskillen	Brother of Rev. Alexander Osborne (387)
1424	Ostler	Thomas	Co. Monaghan	
1657	Ouverquerke	General	Holland	With a great reputation for bravery he accompanied King William in his campaigns in Ireland and Flanders.
1425	Owens	Blayney	Co. Monaghan	
1426	Owens	Edward	Co. Monaghan	
1427	Oyster	Sergeant John	Co. Monaghan	
1428	Oyster	Sergeant John	Co. Cavan	
1373	Page	not recorded	Co. Armagh	
1231	Pallent	James	Co. Down	
1230	Palmer	William	Co. Down	
1505	Palmer	Rev. James	Co. Leitrim	
261	Parker	Colonel	Coleraine	Deserted to the Jacobite camp on 25 April 1689.
1159	Parmetter	Nicholas	Killygordon, Donegal	
1429	Parr	James	Co. Monaghan	
1430	Parry	Richard	Co. Monaghan	
1564	Parsons	William	Enniskillen	
1160	Paton	Henry	Ramelton, Donegal	
772	Pearse	Henry	Derry	Admitted a Freeman of the city of Derry on 2 November 1692
1494	Perrot	John	Co. Cavan	
126	Phillips	George	Limavady, Co. Derry	In Derry during Siege of 1641. Inherited from his father Captain Sir Thomas Phillips, the O'Kanes ancient castle and estate at Limavady. Sir Thomas Phillips had come to Ulster in the Elizabethan wars with Tyrone.
127	Phillips	Paulett	Limavady, Co. Derry	Son of George Phillips (126)
128	Phillips	Captain Thomas	Limavady, Co. Derry	Son of George Phillips (126)
129	Phillips	Dudley	Limavady, Co. Derry	Son of George Phillips (126)
1628	Pitts	Mary	Derry	
1319	Pockridge	Edward	Gortnachige, Co. Fermanagh	
1320	Pockridge	Richard	Co. Monaghan	A family long settled in Enniskillen and neighbourhood

Young's ID	Surname	First Name	Residence	Remarks
764	Pogue (or Poke)	Captain Alexandrer	Derry	
765	Pogue (or Poke)	Family	Derry	Alexander Pogue's wife, her mother and brother were killed by a bomb falling on their house
843	Pointz	Captain Charles	Acton, Co. Armagh	Grandson of Sir Charles Pointz of Iron Acton, Gloucestershire who was among the original grantees of lands in Co. Armagh at the Plantation
584	Pollock	Lieutenant William		
433	Ponsonby	Colonel William		Son of Sir John Ponsonby, who came to Ireland with Cromwell in 1649, and acquired a large estate in the south of Ireland
566	Pooler	Robert	Tyross	
1629	Poore	William	Derry	
524	Porter	Robert	Burt, Co. Donegal	Slew 9 Irish soldiers at Battle of Windmill Hill on 4 June 1689
1431	Ports	Thomas	Co. Monaghan	
1087	Powell	Jonathan	Londonderry	
1088	Powell	Margaret	Derry	
1495	Pratt	Berry	Co. Cavan	
1496	Pratt	Joseph	Co. Cavan	
230	Price	Nicholas	Hollymount, Co. Down	Son of Richard Price, an army officer, who was residing in Newry by 1659 and was Sheriff of Co. Down in 1666.
231	Price	William	Donegal or Londonderry	
232	Price	John	Co. Cavan	
1626	Price	Thomas	Derry	
1627	Price	Humphrey	Derry	
1232	Pringle	William	Co. Down	
1161	Quelsh (Welsh)	Captain John	Donegal	
1374	Radcliff	Hugh	Co. Armagh	
1375	Radcliff	Alick	Derry	
643	Ragston	William		
586	Railey	Ensign John		
583	Ranke	Lieutenant Edward		
341	Rankin	Martha	Derry	Daughter of widow, Margaret Rankin who married Captain Browning (340). Martha married John Harvey of Malin Head in 1685
342	Rankin	Lieutenant		
343	Rankin	Alick		
344	Rankin	John	Derry	
34	Rawdon	Sir Arthur	Moira, Co. Down	Son of Sir George Rawdon who held the large estate of Moria, Co. Down
1162	Rea	Captain James	Donegal	
517	Read	Lieutenant Michael		
519	Read	Major John	Co. Armagh	
1233	Redmond	William	Co. Down	
518	Reid	Alexander	Derry	
1163	Reney	Captain Hugh	Londonderry	
546	Rice	Captain Edmond		
175	Richard	Colonel Solomon		Commander of English Regiment that arrived in the Foyle on 15 April 1689 but returned to England on 18th April without landing stores and munitions. Court-martialed
825	Richards	Captain		An engineer officer with General Kirke's relieving force
1460	Richards	John	Co. Cavan	Yeoman
1063	Richardson	William	Londonderry	Agent of Merchant Taylors' estate near Coleraine. Purchased Somerset estate in 1726.

Young's ID	Surname	First Name	Residence	Remarks
1064	Richardson	Henry	Co. Monaghan	High Sheriff of Co. Monaghan. First of the family settled in Monaghan from Norfolk in Elizabeth's reign and acquired the Poplar Vale estate from Charles II in 1667.
1065	Richardson	Alexander	Co. Tyrone	
1066	Richardson	Archibald	Co. Tyrone	
1067	Richardson	William	Co. Tyrone	
538	Rickaby	Captain		
221	Ridgeway	Winston	England	3rd Earl of Londonderry. Grandson of Sir Thomas Ridgeway who secured a considerable portion of land in Co. Tyrone at the Plantation, and had obtained Earldom of Londonderry in 1622.
1234	Ringland	John	Co. Down	
1632	Ripley	Mathew	Derry	
1528	Roberts	John	Enniskillen	
1048	Robertson	Margaret	Derry	
1631	Robin	Ann	Derry	
1032	Robinson	Henry	Ballyclegan, Co. Monaghan	
1033	Robinson	George senior	Co. Monaghan	
1034	Robinson	George junior	Co. Monaghan	
1035	Robinson	William	Co. Monaghan	
1036	Robinson	William	Co. Monaghan	
1037	Robinson	George	Co. Fermanagh	
1038	Robinson	Henry	Co. Fermanagh	
1039	Robinson	George	Co. Down	
1040	Robinson	John	Co. Cavan	
1041	Robinson	Mark	Co. Cavan	
1042	Robinson	Joseph	Enniskillen	
1044	Robinson	James	Enniskillen	
1045	Robinson	Richard	Enniskillen	
373	Robison	Rev. Andrew	Stewartstown, Co. Tyrone	Curate of Stewartstown, Diocese of Armagh
1043	Robison	Robert	Enniskillen	Probably descendants of Robinsons who were settled for several generations at Mulleghy near Enniskillen
1046	Robison	James	Derry	
1047	Robison	Robert	Derry	
708	Roche	Lieutenant		
668	Rock	James		Messenger of the relieving force who swam up the river. Captured
1630	Roe	Elizabeth	Derry	Signaller to the relief fleet by hoisting flag on St Columb's Cathedral
488	Rogers	Captain Robert		
489	Rogers	William	Derry	
490	Rogers	Thomas	Derry	
1553	Rosecrow	Thomas	Enniskillen	Grandson of William Rosecrow, Provost of Enniskillen in 1618
1321	Rosgrave	Thomas	Toridonochie, Co. Fermanagh	
876	Ross	Captain David	Derry	This family long settled in Co. Derry, chiefly at Limavady
877	Ross	Andrew	Derry	
878	Ross	James	Derry	
879	Ross	Francis	Co. Monaghan	
880	Ross	Robert	Co. Down	
881	Ross	James	Co. Down	
882	Ross	Hugh	Rossgagh, Co. Tyrone	
883	Ross	Rev. Robert	Co. Leitrim	
1164	Rossal	David	Londonderry	

Young's ID	Surname	First Name	Residence	Remarks
378	Rowan	Rev. John	Balteagh, Co. Derry	Rector of Balteagh, Diocese of Derry. Died in the city during the siege
907	Rowan	Rev. Andrew	Clough, Co. Antrim	Settled in Ireland from Scotland. Incumbent of Old Stone (Donaghy), Clough from 1661. The Rowans of Mount Davys are descended from Rev. Andrew Rowan.
908	Rowan	Captain William		
382	Rowat (or Ruitt)	Rev. John	Lifford, Co. Donegal	Presbyterian minister of Lifford
448	Rowley	Hugh	Castleroe, Co. Derry	Descended from John Rowley, a leading merchant in London, who came to Ulster in 1610 as agent for City of London, acquired considerable property in Castleroe and became first Mayor of Londonderry in 1613.
578	Royde	Ensign James		
1512	Royse	Richard	Derry	
1526	Rullock	Michael	Derry	
1497	Russell	George	Co. Cavan	
1376	Rutthorne	Joseph	Co. Armagh	
1658	Ruvigny	The Marquis of	France	A Huguenot. This French soldier went into exile with his fellow Huguenots, in 1690, and entered the service of King William as a major-general, thereby forfeiting his French estates. He served in William's campaigns in Ireland and Flanders. In recognition of his services he was created Earl of Galway.
563	Ruxton	Captain William	Co. Louth	Son of John Ruxton of Ardee House, Co. Louth
1014	Ryder	Captain John	Co. Monaghan	Assisted in preparations for defence of Enniskillen
1322	Rynd	David	Dewslish, Co. Fermanagh	Provost of Enniskillen in 1682. A family long settled in Enniskillen and district.
726	Sampson	Colonel Michael	Fahan, Co. Donegal	Owner of Burt and Inch Castle. Son of Major Richard Sampson who, at the Plantation, acquired considerable estate at Burt.
727	Sampson	Michael		
728	Sampson	Michael		
1235	Sanders	John	Co. Down	
1639	Sankey	Thomas	Derry	Thomas Sankey for Jeremima Sankey
304	Saunderson	Alexander	Tullylagan, Co. Cavan	Grandson of Alexander Saunderson who came from Scotland to Ulster in 1613 and obtained a grant of the Tullylagan estate which became the manor of Castle Saunderson and son of Archibald Saunderson
305	Saunderson	Alexander	Tullylagan, Co. Cavan	Son of Alexander Saunderson (304)
306	Saunderson	Captain Archibald	Tullylagan, Co. Cavan	
307	Saunderson	Colonel Robert	Portagh, Castle Saunderson, Co. Cavan	Grandson of Alexander Saunderson who came from Scotland to Ulster in 1613 and obtained a grant of the Tullylagan estate which became the manor of Castle Saunderson and son of Robert Saunderson
1646	Savage	Captain Hugh	Ardkeen, The Ards, Co. Down	Son of John Savage of Ardkeen. Officer in King William's army. This ancient Anglo-Norman family is descended from Sir William Le Sauvage, one of the knights who accompanied John de Courcy in his invasion of north-east Ulster in 1177.
248	Schomberg	Duke		Descended from an old and noble family in the Palatinate (Germany).
249	Schomberg	Count Meinhardt		Son of Duke of Schomberg (248)
971	Scimin (Simond)	Gunner Quartermaster		
993	Scot	John	Co. Donegal	
994	Scot	Mathew	Kinore, Co. Donegal or Londonderry	
995	Scot	Robert	Co. Monaghan	
996	Scot	Robert	Co. Monaghan	
997	Scot	William	Co. Monaghan	
998	Scot	George	Co. Monaghan	
1551	Scot	Thomas	Enniskillen	

Young's ID	Surname	First Name	Residence	Remarks
1552	Scot	Ninian	Enniskillen	
999	Scott	Jean	Derry	
1000	Scott	Rev. Gideon		Chaplain in one of King William's regiments and purchased the estate of Willsborough (near Eglinton), Co. Derry in 1696
1432	Scouts	John	Co. Monaghan	
370	Sempill	Rev. Thomas	Donaghmore, Co. Donegal	Rector of Donaghmore, Diocese of Derry
1433	Sharpe	John	Co. Monaghan	
54	Shaw	Colonel William	Bush, Co. Antrim	Descended from ancient Scottish family. The Shaws originally settled on the Montgomery estate at Ards, Co. Down
55	Shaw	Patrick	Ballygalley Castle, Co. Antrim	Brother of Colonel William Shaw (54)
56	Shaw	Henry	Ballyvoy, near Ballycastle, Co. Antrim	Grandson of Colonel William Shaw (54)
57	Shaw	Charles	Co. Antrim	
58	Shaw	William	Gemmeway, Co. Antrim	
59	Shaw	William	Co. Down	
60	Shaw	James	Belfast	
577	Shelcross	Ensign Samuel		
1636	Shenles	Jean	Derry	
664	Shennan	Robert		
273	Sherard	Bennet	Leitrim	2nd Baron Sherard, his father had been created Baron in 1627 by Charles I
274	Sherard	Daniel		One of 13 apprentice boys who shut the gates on 7 December 1688.
275	Sherard	William		One of 13 apprentice boys who shut the gates on 7 December 1688.
276	Sherard	Robert		
277	Sherard	Orphans of Mrs Hutton		
1542	Sheriffe	John	Enniskillen	
251	Shoburn	Anthony		
1323	Shore	Gabriel	Magheraghoy, Co. Fermanagh	
1324	Shore	Thomas	Co. Fermanagh	
557	Shortridge	Ensign Forest	Co. Antrim	
250	Shumberg	Anthony		
389	Sinclair	Rev. John	Holyhill, Co. Donegal	Grandson of Sir James Sinclair of Caithness, Scotland and son of James Sinclair who was the first of the name in Co. Donegal. Rector of Leckpatrick. His church was burnt by the Jacobite army on their retreat from Derry
390	Sinclair	James	Ramelton, Donegal or Londonderry	
24	Skeffington	Sir John	Antrim Castle, Co. Antrim	2nd Viscount Massereene of Lough Neagh and Antrim Castle. The first of the name in Ireland was Sir William Skeffington who came to Dublin in 1539
25	Skeffington	Colonel Clothworthy	Antrim Castle, Co. Antrim	3rd Viscount Massereene, son of Sir John Skeffington
1549	Skelton	Richard	Enniskillen	
1550	Skelton	Ichabod	Enniskillen	
754	Skinner	Robert		
755	Skinner	James		
844	Skipton	Captain Alexander	Donegal or Londonderry	This family, originating in Hungtingdonshire, England, were of considerable importance in the city of Derry, owning Ballyshasky (Beech Hill), Glendermot Parish. John Skipton was Mayor in 1670.
845	Skipton	Captain George	Donegal or Londonderry	
846	Skipton	Captain George	Donegal or Londonderry	
1378	Skipworth	Not recorded	Co. Armagh	
1325	Slack	John	Monaghan	
1326	Slack	William	Enniskillen, Co. Fermanagh	
1635	Slater	Katherine	Derry	
1236	Smart	John	Co. Down	

Young's ID	Surname	First Name	Residence	Remarks
687	Smith	James		Shot on wall near Butcher's Gate.
688	Smith	Thomas		
689	Smith	Captain William	Londonderry	
690	Smith	Captain Ralph	Co. Antrim	
691	Smith	Captain David	Belfast, Co. Antrim	
692	Smith	Erasmus	Armagh	
693	Smith	Erasmus	Armagh	
694	Smith	John	Co. Down	
695	Smith	Roger	Co. Monaghan	
696	Smith	Rev. William	Co. Monaghan	
697	Smith	William	Co. Monaghan	
698	Smith	William	Co. Monaghan	
699	Smith	Rev. William	Clenish, Co. Fermanagh	
700	Smith	William	Greenich, Co. Fermanagh	
701	Smith	William	Clenish, Co. Fermanagh	
702	Smith	Henry		
703	Smith	Joseph		
1079	Smith	William	Co. Donegal	Bishop of Raphoe
1655	Solmes	Count	Holland	Commanded the Dutch forces at the Battle of the Boyne. Killed at the Battle of Landen, in William's Flanders campaign, in 1693.
1434	Sparks	John	Co. Monaghan	
1200	Speere	John	Tyrone	
1201	Speere	John	Tyrone	Probably son of John Speere (1200)
1165	Spence	Patrick	Donegal or Londonderry	
1199	Spence	John	Tyrone	
833	Spike (or Spaight)	Lieutenant James	Londonderry	One of 13 apprentice boys who shut the gates on 7 December 1688. Resided at Coleraine after the siege. The first of the name came from Woolwich.
1435	Springland	William	Co. Monaghan	
676	Squire	Alderman Gervais	Donaghmore, Co. Donegal	Ceased to be an alderman when Tyrconnell revoked the old charter in 1688. Mayor of Derry in 1675, 1676 and 1690.
677	Squire	William		Mayor of Derry in 1692
1377	St. John	Oliver	Co. Armagh	
102	Stafford	Edmund	Mount Stafford, Portglenone, Co. Antrim	His great-grandfather, Sir Francis Stafford, acquired large estates in Portglenone area.
737	Stanley	William	Derry	One of 4 Protestant Burgesses appointed by Tyrconnell to the new Corporation of Derry in 1688.
943	Staples	Sir Robert	Lissan, Co. Tyrone	Descended from Thomas Staples who, at the Plantation, received a grant of the Lissan estate.
944	Staples	Mathew	Lissan, Co. Tyrone	
1068	Steinson	John	Co. Down	
974	Stephens	Oliver senior	Co. Cavan	
975	Stephens	Oliver junior	Co. Cavan	
976	Stephens	Thomas	Co. Cavan	
977	Stephens	William	Co. Cavan	
1560	Sterling	Robert	Enniskillen	Lieutenant in local force
838	Stevenson	Robert		Artillery officer during the siege
839	Stevenson	Robert	Enniskillen	
938	Steward	James	Derry	
18	Stewart	Sir William	Ramelton, Co. Donegal	One of 13 apprentice boys who shut the gates on 7 December 1688. Viscount Mountjoy, created 1685. His grandfather Sir William Stewart was the original Scottish grantee of the Ramelton estate at the time of the Plantation

Young's ID	Surname	First Name	Residence	Remarks
19	Stewart	William	Ramelton, Co. Donegal	Eldest son of Sir William Stewart, Viscount Mountjoy
20	Stewart	Major Alexander	Ramelton, Co. Donegal	second son of Sir William Stewart, Viscount Mountjoy
222	Stewart	Colonel William	Ballylawn, Co. Donegal	The first of the family in Donegal was John Stewart who had a grant of Ballylawn in Charles I's reign
223	Stewart	Thomas	Ballylawn, Co. Donegal	Son of Colonel William Stewart (222)
926	Stewart	William	Killymoon, Co. Tyrone	William Stewart and Rev. George Walker defended Dungannon before marching their men to Derry.
927	Stewart	James	Killymoon, Co. Tyrone	
928	Stewart	William	Co. Tyrone	
929	Stewart	John	Dundaff, Co. Donegal	Son or grandson of William Stewart, Laird of Dundaff, Ayrshire, Scotland who received land in Co. Donegal
930	Stewart	Alexander	Co. Down	
931	Stewart	Alexander	Co. Down	
932	Stewart	Patrick	Drumskeeny, Co. Tyrone	
933	Stewart	Colonel Charles	Ballintoy, Co. Antrim	The Stewarts, descended from Robert II of Scotland and the hereditary Sheriffs of Bute, settled on the territory of the Macdonnells of the Glens, near Ballintoy on the Antrim coast, about 1560. One of 23 gentry of Co. Antrim who raised regiments in defence of Protestant interests in the county.
934	Stewart	Captain William	Ballintoy, Co. Antrim	
935	Stewart	James	Ballylusk, Co. Antrim	
939	Stewart	Marmion		
940	Stewart	Jennet	Derry	
1514	Stiles	James	Derry	
1634	Stinnie	Robert	Derry	
1069	Stinsome	John	Derry	Probably same person as 1068; Refugee in Derry.
1633	Stinsome	John	Derry	
678	Stone	James	Co. Down	
679	Stone	Edmund		
1637	Stott	Enery	Derry	
1638	Stott	Enery	Derry	
312	Strong	John	Cavan	
311	Strong	James	Cavan	
309	Stronge	Mathew	Clonlea, Donegal or Londonderry	Descended from Strang or Strong of Balcaskie, Fifeshire, Scotland, Mathew Stronge first settled at Strabane (Co. Tyrone) in 1670 and at Clonlea (Lifford, Co. Donegal) in 1683.
310	Stronge	Captain James	Clonlea, Donegal or Londonderry	Son of Mathew Stronge (309). Strong's Orchard, 80 perches in size outside the city walls, was selected by the besiegers as a position for their big guns. The Stronges of Tynan Abbey, Co. Armagh were descendants.
41	Stroud	Major Joseph	Lisburn, Co. Down	
925	Stuart	Hugh	Gortgall, Co. Tyrone	The first of the family in Co. Tyrone was Andrew Stuart, 2nd Baron of Ochiltree, Scotland, who received, at the Plantation, a considerable grant of lands in Co. Tyrone and became Baron Castlestewart
936	Stuart	William	Co. Cavan	Grandson of Robert Stuart, a kinsman of James I, who, at the Plantation, received a considerable grant of lands in Co. Cavan. Fought at the Boyne and Limerick and rose to the rank of Brigadier-General. After the Williamite Wars he was forced to sell his estate as impoverished by the raising and equipping of his regiment, the 9th Regiment of Foot.
937	Stuart	Henry		Nephew of William Stuart (936)
1533	Summes	Oylett	Enniskillen	
Young's ID	Surname	First Name	Residence	Remarks

Young's ID	Surname	First Name	Residence	Remarks
1202	Swan	William	Turlough, Tyrone	
260	Swanzy	Ensign Henry	Aveireagh, Clontibret, Co. Monaghan	Son of Henry Swanzy of Blaris, Co. Down
1166	Sweetman	Tristram	Burt, Donegal or Londonderry	
1167	Sweetman	George	Burt, Donegal or Londonderry	
1237	Swift	Robert	Co. Down	
1654	Talmash	General	England	Served with distinction in William's Irish campaign at Athlone and Aughrim. Noted for his gallantry in covering the retreat of William's defeated army at Steinkirk, in the Flanders campaign, in 1692. Died from his wounds, leading an invasion army of 10,000 soldiers, in the unsuccesful attempt to capture the Frecnh port of Brest in 1694.
1203	Tate	Adam	Ballygawley, Tyrone	
1461	Tate	Joseph	Co. Cavan	Yeoman
786	Taylor	Captain		
787	Taylor	Richard	Enniskillen	
1498	Terman	John	Co. Cavan	
1379	Thacker	Gilbert	Co. Armagh	
1436	Thomas	Robert	Co. Monaghan	
1437	Thomas	Christopher	Derry	
749	Thompson	Alderman Henry	Derry	Killed by a bomb on 5 June 1689
750	Thompson	Lieutenant Henry	Londonderry	
751	Thompson	Thomas	Derry	
752	Thompson	Captain Thomas	Derry	
753	Thompson	William	Derry	Descendant of Hugh Thompson, Sheriff of city in 1623
1640	Thorn	Thomas	Derry	
1438	Thornton	George	Co. Monaghan	
1439	Thornton	Joseph	Co. Monaghan	
1440	Thornton	Thomas	Co. Monaghan	
636	Tomkins	Alderman Alexander	Derry	Prominent citizen of Derry and landowner atTirkearing, Co. Donegal. Ceased to be an alderman when Tyrconnell revoked the old charter in 1688. Raised a regiment from his Tirkearing tenantry and neighbours to defend Derry.
637	Tomkins	Captain John	Derry	Son of Alderman Alexander Tomkins (636)
638	Tomkins	George	Derry	Mayor of Derry in 1706, Agent of Irish Society and M.P. for the city in 1715. Buried in the Cathedral.
1441	Torren	William	Co. Monaghan	
834	Torrens	John	Derry	The Torrens family were later to marry into the Richardson family who had purchased the Somerset estate (Coleraine) from the Merchant Taylors' Company in 1726.
1499	Townley	Samuel	Co. Cavan	
553	Tracey	Captain Thomas		
554	Tracey	James		
1380	Trenchard	William	Co. Armagh	
1381	Trenchard	William	Co. Armagh	Son of William Trenchard (1380)
234	Trevor	Colonel Sir Marcus	Rostrevor, Co. Down	Ardent supporter of Charles I during English civil war and created, at Restortaion, Viscount Dungannon in 1662.
1168	Trueman	Ralph	Londonderry	
823	Tubman	Lieutenant	Antrim	
1238	Turk	Richard	Co. Down	
35	Upton	Arthur	Castle Upton, Co. Antrim	The first of the family in Co. Antrim was Henry Upton of Devonshire
36	Upton	Clothworthy	Castle Upton, Co. Antrim	Son of Arthur Upton (35)
37	Upton	Arthur	Castle Upton, Co. Antrim	Son of Arthur Upton (35)

Young's ID	Surname	First Name	Residence	Remarks
38	Upton	Oliver	Castle Upton, Co. Antrim	
1641	Vaile	John	Derry	
1382	Valentine	Thomas	Co. Armagh	
263	Vance	Lancelot	Coagh, Co. Tyrone	Surgeon. Died of excessive fatigue during the siege.
264	Vance	Colonel Patrick	Bamburragh, Wigtonshire, Scotland	Son of Sir John Vans of Bamburragh, Wigtonshire
299	Vaughan	George	Buncrana, Co. Donegal	Desended from Sir John Vaughan a grantee at the Plantation of considerable estate at Buncrana, Co. Donegal. In 1611 he was appointed Governor of Derry, which he held until his death in 1641.
300	Vaughan	Captain George	Co. Donegal or Londonderry	
301	Vaughan	Charles	Armagh	
302	Vaughan	Major		
303	Vaughan	Lieutenant Robert	Enniskillen	
1506	Vernloe	Thomas	Co. Leitrim	
1462	Voss	Bryan	Co. Cavan	Yeoman
1507	Waagle	Not recorded	Co. Leitrim	
1239	Waddle	James	Co. Down	
1500	Waldron	Henry	Co. Cavan	
3	Walker	Rev. George	Donoughmore, Co. Tyrone	Episcopalian minister. Governor of Derry from 19 April 1689. His story of the 'Siege' was published. Died at Battle of the Boyne
4	Walker	William	Donoughmore, Co. Tyrone	Son of Governor George Walker. Descendants of a Nottinghamshire family.
6	Walker	George	Donoughmore, Co. Tyrone	Son of Governor George Walker. Descendants of a Nottinghamshire family.
5	Walker	Robert	Donoughmore, Co. Tyrone	Son of Governor George Walker. Descendants of a Nottinghamshire family.
1240	Walkingham	Rev. Mungo	Down	
572	Wallace	Captain William	Londonderry	
573	Wallace	Hugh	Ravera, Co. Down	
574	Wallace	John	Ravera, Co. Down	
575	Wallace	Robert		
1442	Walsh	Joseph	Co. Monaghan	
1443	Walsh	Sergeant Thomas	Co. Monaghan	
1444	Walton	Henry	Leghlenagalgrene, Co. Monaghan	
1445	Walton	William	Leghlenalgrene, Co. Monaghan	
375	Walworth	Rev. James	Errigal, Co. Derry	Rector of Errigal, Diocese of Derry. Died in the city during the siege
1057	Ward	Bernard	Castleward, Co. Down	Great-grandson of Sir Thomas Ward of Cheshire, Surveyor-General of Ireland in 1570, who settled in Co. Down and bought the Castleward estate.
1058	Ward	John	Castleward, Co. Down	
1059	Ward	Charles	Killyleagh, Co. Down	
1060	Ward	Bernard	Co. Fermanagh	
1061	Ward	Captain Bernard	Carrick, Co. Monaghan	
1062	Ward	Bryan	Co. Monaghan	
1529	Ward	Robert	Enniskillen	
1463	Wardell	William	Co. Cavan	Yeoman
1242	Wardlaw	Jean	Derry	
1241	Wardlow	Thomas	Down	
1015	Waring	Samuel	Waringstown, Co. Down	Sheriff of Co. Down in 1690 and M.P. for Hillsborough 1703-1715. Grandson of William Waring of Lancashire who settled in Co. Down early in 17th century and son of John Waring who purchased the Waringstown estate in 1656.
1256	Waring	Roger	Belfast, Co. Antrim	
1243	Warren	Richard	Co. Down	
1244	Warren	Thomas	Co. Down	
1447	Warren	Rev. William	Co. Monaghan	

Young's ID	Surname	First Name	Residence	Remarks
1383	Warwick	William	Co. Armagh	
1384	Warwick	Purefoy	Co. Armagh	Captain of the Gunners (in charge of 200 gunners and 20 cannon) and Chief Engineer of the garrison
493	Watson	Captain Alexander		
494	Watson	George	Enniskillen	
1446	Watson	Roger	Enniskillen, Co. Fermanagh	
1385	Watts	William	Co. Armagh	
1329	Wear	Alexander	Mumaghan, Co. Fermanagh	
1330	Wear	Robert	Enniskillen, Co. Fermanagh	
1086	Webb	Rev. Ezekiel	Enniskillen	Incumbent of Enniskillen
1327	Webster	John	Co. Monaghan	
1328	Webster	Mathew	Enniskillen, Co. Fermanagh	
1643	Welsh	William	Derry	
1245	West	Henry	Co. Down	
1448	West	John	Co. Monaghan	
1642	Westgate	John	Derry	
817	Whalley	Colonel Richard		
224	White	Rev. Fulke	Whitehall, Broughshane, Co. Antrim	Settled in Broughshane in 1650 and was the first Presbyterian minister of Broughshane
437	White	Colonel Robert	England?	Died 5 August 1689.
438	White	Ensign John	Co. Tyrone	
439	White	Thomas	Co. Cavan	
440	White	David	Co. Down	
441	White	Nicholas		
442	White	Francis	Co. Tyrone	
443	White	Francis	Co. Cavan	
444	White	George	Derry	
445	White	Thomas	Derry	
391	Whitney	Colonel Thomas		
366	Whittel	Rev. Seth	Bellaghy, Co. Derry	Rector of Bellaghy, Diocese of Derry. Died in the city during the siege
1644	Whyt	Robert	Derry	
1645	Whyt	Mary	Derry	
393	Wigton	Lieutenant-Colonel John	Raphoe, Co. Donegal	
1449	Wilcocks	William	Co. Monaghan	
1450	Wildman	John	Skeogh, Co. Monaghan	
1451	Wildman	Thomas	Skeogh, Co. Monaghan	
1517	Wilkins	Benjamin	Derry	
1204	Williams	John	Tyrone	
1205	Williams	William	Derry	
1386	Williamson	Joseph	Co. Armagh	
384	Wilson	Rev. Robert	Strabane, Co. Tyrone	Presbyterian minister of Strabane. Died in the city during the siege
741	Wilson	Captain Frank		
742	Wilson	James		
743	Wilson	Ensign John		
744	Wilson	Ensign Joseph	Tullywilson, Co. Longford	
745	Wilson	Hugh	Co. Tyrone	
746	Wilson	Hugh	Co. Tyrone	
747	Wilson	John	Co. Tyrone	
748	Wilson	John	Rashie, Co. Antrim	
1452	Winslow	Thomas	Gerrygore, Co. Monaghan	Supposed to have landed at Carrickfergus in 1690 with King William

Young's ID	Surname	First Name	Residence	Remarks
1080	Wiseman	Capell	Co. Down	Bishop of Dromore
1331	Wishard	Captain William	Clontivern, Co. Monaghan	Raised a troop of horse to support the men of Enniskillen. Son of Sir John Wishardt, Laird of Pettaro, Scotland who, at the Plantation, was granted land at Leitrim, Co. Donegal.
1332	Wishart	William	Co. Fermanagh	
964	Wolseley	Colonel William	Enniskillen	Son of Sir Robert Wolseley of Wolseley, Staffordshire, England. Led, with distinction, the men of Enniskillen at Newtonbutler and the Boyne.
870	Wood	Edward	Derry	
872	Wood	Archibald	Co. Armagh	
875	Wood	Edward	Court, Co. Sligo	
871	Woods	Captain Edward	Ballyshannon	Became prominent family in Enniskillen
873	Woods	Alexander	Co. Tyrone	
874	Woods	William	Co. Cavan	
1169	Workman	Meredith	Londonderry	
1021	Wray	Humphrey	Co. Armagh	
1022	Wray	William	Castleroe, Donegal or Londonderry	The first of the name in Co. Donegal was John Wray who, in 1620, purchased from Sir John Vaughan the lands of Carnegill (1000 acres) near Castleroe
598	Wright	Captain Sam	Londonderry or Donegal	
599	Wright	James	Co. Monaghan	
600	Wright	James	Co. Monaghan	
601	Wright	Sergeant John	Co. Monaghan	
602	Wright	Richard	Co. Monaghan	
603	Wright	John		
604	Wright	James		Descendants of this family residing near Ballinrode, Co. Monaghan in 19th century
740	Wurtemberg	Duke Frederick of		Commander of Danish army of 6000 which landed near Carrickfergus before the Boyne
965	Wynne	Captain James	Hazlewood, Co. Sligo	Commanded, with distinction at Enniskillen and the Boyne, one of the Dragoon regiments raised by the men of Enniskillen in July 1689. First of the family in Ireland was Owen Wynne of Wales who settled in Co. Sligo in Queen Elizabeth's reign.
225	Young	James	Balluchchule, Co. Donegal	Son of Rev John Young of Scottish descent, Rector of Urney in middle of 17th century; Youngs of Coolkeeragh descend from this line. Youngs of Culdaff descend from Rev. Robert Young of Devonshire who was appointed Rector of Cloncha in 1640 and of Culdaff in 1668.
226	Young	Mathew	Enniskillen	
226	Young	Thomas	Enniskillen	
227	Young	James	Cavan	
228	Young	James	Co. Tyrone	
229	Young	James	Co. Monaghan	
587	Young	Ensign John		
822	Zachariah	Major		Officer of relieving force

www.ingramcontent.com/pod-product-compliance
Lightning Source LLC
Chambersburg PA
CBHW081136170426
43197CB00017B/2880